MW01716697

Bold Blueprint

A high school guide to vision, purpose, and action

Your Guide to College, Career, and Life on Your Own Terms

Also by Cecilia Hegamin-Younger

Being Bold and Driven: The Challenges and Victories of Building a Business

Being Bold Journal

Bold Blueprint

A high school guide to vision, purpose, and action

Your Guide to College, Career, and Life on Your Own Terms

Cecilia Hegamin-Younger, PhD

Copyright © Cecilia Hegamin-Younger

All rights reserved.

No part of this publication may be reproduced, stored in a retrieval system, or transmitted in any form or by any means, without the prior permission in writing of the publisher, nor be otherwise circulated in any form of binding or cover other than that in which it is published and without a similar condition including this condition being imposed on the subsequent publisher.

ISBN: 978-0-9997177-5-2

Contents

Table of Contents

Bold Blueprint

A high school guide to vision, purpose, and action

A Note to You

This book was written for you ... the student standing at the edge of everything.

Maybe you are a junior or senior in high school, staring down the last stretch before graduation and trying to figure out what comes next. Maybe you have college applications open on your laptop and a creeping uncertainty about which direction to go. Maybe you already know, with a quiet certainty, that you want to start a business or jump straight into the workforce. Or maybe , and this is the most honest option , you have absolutely no idea what you want, and that uncertainty is sitting heavy on your chest.

Whatever your situation, this book is for you. All of you. The one who has it figured out, the one who absolutely does not, and the one who thinks they have it figured out but secretly wonders if they are on the right track. You are all the same person at different moments.

Being Bold and Driven was originally written for professionals building careers in business. The research behind it came from more than 100 in-depth interviews with entrepreneurs and executives across the country, people who had already been in the arena, who had built things, lost things, rebuilt things, and eventually figured out what the difference between thriving and struggling actually looked like from the inside.

But as I studied what those conversations revealed, I kept arriving at the same uncomfortable realization: the lessons did not just apply to adults already in their careers. They applied to anyone at the starting line. And the most frustrating part was that most of the people I interviewed had learned these lessons the hard way. Nearly all of them said some version of the same thing: I wish someone had told me this when I was young.

That phrase became this book.

I want to tell you about one interview that changed the way I thought about this project. I was sitting across from a woman who had built a successful regional business over fifteen years. She was sharp, thoughtful, and generous with her time. About an hour into our conversation, I asked her what she would tell her younger self if she could go back. She was quiet for a long moment. Then she said: I would tell her that the technical knowledge would come. That you could always learn the tools. But that I wasted years not understanding how to show up for people, not knowing how to find and use a mentor, not having any real picture of where I was trying to go. I was working incredibly hard and going in circles.

That interview was typical, not exceptional. I heard some version of that reflection in interview after interview. The pattern was so consistent that it became impossible to ignore: the people who were struggling had almost universally neglected the intangibles. Not out of laziness or bad intentions, but simply because nobody had ever told them these things existed, let alone taught them how to build them.

This book is an attempt to correct that. To say, before you have paid the price of learning these things the hard way: here is what the research found. Here is what the people who thrived did differently. Here is what you can start doing right now, before any of the professional and life stakes are real, to build the invisible infrastructure that will hold everything else up.

The skills separating people who thrive from those who struggle are not primarily technical skills from a classroom. They are the intangibles: how you show up in the world, who you build genuine relationships with, how clearly you can see where you want to go, how honestly you know yourself, and how intentionally you invest across the different dimensions of your life. These are learnable skills. Every one of them. They are not personality traits you are born with or social advantages that belong to someone else. And you can start building them right now.

Here is what this book is not. It is not a list of motivational quotes. It is not a shortcut. It is not a substitute for hard work, for dealing honestly with failure, or for the patience required to build anything real. The intangibles are not magic. They are infrastructure, invisible, unsexy, quietly essential foundations that either hold everything else up or don't.

Here is what this book is. It is the honest distillation of lessons that took real people years of trial and error to learn. It is a framework for thinking about your own development in a more systematic, more intentional way. And it is a genuine invitation: to take your own future seriously, starting today, before you have paid the price of learning these things the hard way.

You do not have to have everything figured out to read this book. You just have to be willing to think honestly and boldly about who you are becoming. That is the only requirement.

— Dr. Cecilia Hegamin-Younger

CHAPTER 1

Who Are You Becoming?

The most important question you can ask yourself right now isn't "what do I want to be?", it's "who am I becoming?"

A few years ago, I set out to answer what seemed like a simple question: why do some people in business thrive while others, with the same training, the same tools, and sometimes the same amount of time invested, struggle?

I interviewed more than 100 entrepreneurs, business owners, and executives across the country. I sat with people at every stage of their journey: those just starting out and barely keeping the lights on, those at the top of their fields, and those somewhere in the uncertain middle, working hard, committed, but not seeing the results they had set out to achieve. I listened carefully to their stories. I asked hard questions. I looked for patterns.

What I found was both surprising and clarifying. The difference between the people who were building something meaningful and those who were struggling had almost nothing to do with how much they knew or how technically skilled they were. They all knew how to do their work. They had comparable training and tools. The gap was not in any of those places.

The gap was in the intangibles.

The thriving group had developed invisible habits, behaviors, and investments that laid a strong foundation under everything they were building. The struggling group, through no particular failure of intelligence or effort, had not. And because nobody had ever explicitly taught those things, the people who lacked them often had no idea what they were missing.

Here is what that has to do with you: you are at the exact moment in your life where those invisible foundations are being formed. Right now. Whether you realize it or not. Whether you are intentional about it or not. Every relationship you invest in or neglect, every habit you build or fail to build, every choice you make about how you show up in the world, all of it is laying the groundwork for who you are going to become. This book is about making that process conscious. About turning an accident into a decision.

I want to offer you a reframe that changed how I understood all of this research. Most conversations about success focus on what people do. This book is about who people are becoming. There is a difference. Doing is transactional: I take this action, I get this result. Becoming is cumulative: I build this habit, I develop this relationship, I invest in this vision, and over time, I become a different kind of person, one capable of doing things and building things I could not have before.

The people I interviewed who were thriving were not, for the most part, people who had done one big impressive thing. They were people who had consistently been a certain kind of person over a long period of time. They showed up. They followed through. They invested in the people around them. They kept their eyes on a direction even when the path was unclear. The results were the inevitable downstream consequence of who they had become. That is the process this book is trying to help you begin.

The Research Behind This Book

The original Being Bold and Driven grew from a specific research design. I identified two groups within the same professional field: people who had been working for roughly the same amount of time but experiencing dramatically different outcomes. One group was struggling. The other were star performers who were building real momentum.

To understand the difference, I went deep. I sat with people, listened to their stories, and asked them to reflect honestly on what had shaped their trajectory. The patterns that emerged were remarkably consistent across every interview, every geography, every demographic background. The thriving group had done specific, describable, learnable things the struggling group had not done. And almost none of those things were technical. Almost all of them were intangibles.

When I looked at those patterns carefully, I realized none of them were adult-specific. They were things you could start building right now, in high school, in the communities and relationships and opportunities you already have access to. That realization is the reason this book exists.

Let me be specific about what the research found, because the specificity matters. In the research behind Being Bold and Driven, the star performers were consistently distinguished from the struggling group by five clusters of intangible behavior. First: they invested in genuine, sustained relationships, not networking for extraction, but community membership for contribution. Second: they had found and actively used real mentors who taught them the unwritten rules of their fields. Third: they presented themselves with intentionality, they understood that how they showed up communicated something, and they chose what to communicate. Fourth: they operated with a clear personal vision that organized their decisions and provided resilience through difficulty. Fifth: they invested deliberately across multiple dimensions of their lives, professional, relational, spiritual, developmental, and civic, rather than sacrificing everything else for career.

Every chapter of this book is built around one of those five clusters. The research behind each chapter is real. The stories in each chapter are drawn from actual interviews with actual people. And the exercises and reflections at the end of each chapter are designed to help you start building what those research subjects built, starting where you are, with what you have, right now.

I want to be honest with you about something: the research behind this book was not done with students in mind. The people I interviewed were adults, many of them with ten, fifteen, or twenty years of professional experience. But the patterns I found were so consistent, and so clearly traceable back to habits formed early in life, that the conclusion was unavoidable. These are not adult problems with adult solutions. They are foundational capacities that can be, and should be, developed long before a person enters their first job or starts their first business.

What follows in this book is not advice invented for students. It is the real, hard-won wisdom of people who built things, and who, almost universally, wished they had started earlier.

Two Types of Knowledge

There are two fundamental types of knowledge that shape how far you go and how well you navigate the road.

Tangible knowledge is measurable, certifiable, and listable: your GPA, your test scores, your degrees, your technical skills. These matter. They open certain doors. You should take them seriously.

Intangible knowledge is the knowledge of how to operate as a person in the world. How to build real, lasting relationships. How to find a mentor and actually learn from them. How to present yourself in ways that build trust. How to develop a clear enough vision to make decisions that move you in a coherent direction. How to align the different dimensions of your life so they reinforce rather than undermine each other.

Most schools teach the first type reasonably well. Almost no school formally teaches the second. The gap between what students leave knowing technically and what they need to know interpersonally and strategically is one of the most consistently costly educational blind spots we have. The students who develop intangible knowledge have an advantage that compounds powerfully over time.

Think about the most successful person you know personally, not a celebrity, but someone in your actual life whose trajectory genuinely impresses you. Now think carefully about why they are successful. Is it primarily their technical knowledge or credentials? Or is it something harder to articulate, the way they carry themselves, the quality of the relationships they have built, the clarity with which they talk about where they are headed? For most genuinely successful people, the intangibles are doing most of the work. The credentials opened the first door. The intangibles built the life.

REAL TALK

Think about two people you know personally who are clearly going in different directions. What actually separates them? In most cases, when you look carefully, it is not primarily intelligence or credentials. It is the intangibles. How they show up. How they treat people. Whether they have a clear sense of direction. Those invisible differences produce very visible results over time.

The Bicycle Wheel: A System, Not a List

Throughout this book I am going to ask you to hold one image in your mind: a bicycle wheel.

What makes a bicycle wheel function is not any one component. It is the integration of all the components working together. The hub. The rim. And the spokes, each one the right length, properly tensioned, doing its specific job. When all the spokes are correctly in place, the wheel has structural integrity. It carries weight. It holds its shape under pressure.

Remove one spoke and the wheel begins to warp. The rim goes out of round. The stress on the remaining spokes causes them to weaken, and eventually they fail too. One missing spoke does not create one isolated problem. It creates a cascade.

Here is a concrete way to see the system in action. Imagine a student, call her Destiny, who has an exceptional academic record and a genuine passion for medicine. She works hard, earns excellent grades, and is clearly intelligent. But she has spent four years of high school almost entirely focused on academic performance. She has no meaningful relationships with adults outside her family. She has never sought out a mentor. She has not developed a vision for her life beyond "I want to go to medical school." She does not know how she comes across to other people.

Now imagine another student, call her Amara, whose GPA is slightly lower. But Amara has invested deeply in one community organization for three years. She has built a genuine relationship with a doctor in her community who has become a real mentor. She has developed a personal vision statement. She thinks carefully about how she shows up in professional contexts. She is genuinely curious and has read widely beyond the curriculum.

In many admission processes, Destiny wins on paper. But in the conversations, the letters of recommendation, the interviews, where character, maturity, and genuine direction become visible, Amara is operating with a completely different foundation. And once both are in professional environments, the gap will only widen. This is the bicycle wheel in practice. Not one spoke. The whole system.

The intangibles work exactly this way. They are not a list of independent tips you can pick and choose from. They are a system. A powerful vision without relationships and mentorship leaves you trying to figure out alone what others could have shown you quickly. A great network without a vision leaves you networking endlessly without building anything. Every chapter of this book is one spoke in the wheel. The system only works when all the spokes are working together.

The bicycle wheel image is also useful for thinking about the difference between maintenance and breakdown. A wheel with all its spokes properly tensioned can handle rough roads, unexpected obstacles, and serious weight. It is resilient because the load is distributed across many strong spokes, each doing its part. The person who has built all the intangibles is similarly resilient. When one area of their life is under stress, a difficult professional period, a relationship challenge, a season of self-doubt, the other areas hold them up. The person who has developed only one or two intangibles has no such resilience. When the spoke they have been relying on fails, the whole wheel collapses.

Three Paths, One Framework

This book is for students heading in three different directions, college, the workforce, or entrepreneurship, and also for those who are not yet sure. The intangibles apply to every path equally because they are the foundations of a meaningful life regardless of its specific shape. Chapter 9 covers the specific applications for each path in depth. But for now, whatever your direction, understand this: the work of building the intangibles starts now. The person you are when you arrive at any threshold will be shaped almost entirely by what you do between now and then.

Many students think of the intangibles as useful for career, but not much else. That is a narrow reading. The capacity for genuine relationship-building matters in your friendships, your family life, your community. A clear personal vision matters for everything from the college you choose to the person you decide to spend time with. The habit of follow-through and reliability matters in every relationship, professional or personal. These are not career tools. They are life tools. Build them now, and every dimension of your life benefits.

A Word About Boldness

Boldness is not loudness. It is not recklessness or the absence of fear. Boldness is the willingness to invest in your future before it is visible. To build relationships before you need them. To develop a vision before it is fully clear. To do the consistent, unglamorous, patient work that most people defer to some vague and never-arriving later. Boldness means showing up, fully and intentionally, to the actual work of becoming who you are capable of becoming. That kind of boldness is available to everyone. It requires only a decision: to take your own future seriously, starting now.

Before we move on, I want to address something directly. You may be reading this from a background with significant disadvantages, financial pressure at home, a school system that has not served you well, a community where the resources described in this book feel out of reach. The intangibles matter even more in those circumstances. Perhaps especially in those circumstances.

The research on social mobility consistently shows that the factors most predictive of upward mobility are intangible ones: the quality of relationships built across class lines, the presence of a mentor who knows how a different world works, the development of a vision specific and compelling enough to sustain effort through real adversity. The intangibles are not advantages reserved for the privileged. They are the great equalizer. They are what every human being, regardless of starting point, can choose to build. And the building of them, done with consistency and genuine investment, narrows the gap between starting point and destination more reliably than almost anything else the research has found.

Most students wait to be bold until the stakes are high and the moment is obvious. The job interview. The college application. The audition. But boldness practiced only in high-stakes moments is fragile, because it has not been trained. The students who are genuinely, reliably bold are those who practice it in small moments ; introducing themselves to someone they do not know, raising a hand when uncertain, taking initiative when nobody asked them to. Small acts of boldness, practiced daily, build a muscle. By the time a genuinely high-stakes moment arrives, the people who have been training consistently step into it with confidence while others freeze.

That is what this book is asking you to do: practice boldness daily, in the small moments, starting now. Not because it is always comfortable. Because it is always worth it.

✎ **REFLECTION, THINK, WRITE, ACT**

1. *When you imagine your life five years from now, what does it look like? Be specific: where are you, what are you doing, who is around you, and how do you feel?*

2. *Think about a person in your life who seems to have things genuinely figured out. What specific habits or behaviors do you notice in them that you want to develop?*

3. *What is one thing you know you should be doing to invest in your future that you keep putting off? What is the real reason?*

4. *Looking at the last thirty days honestly (your habits, your relationships, how you showed up) what kind of foundation have you actually been building? Is it the one you want?*

CHAPTER 2

Building Real Relationships

Your network is not a list of contacts. It is a community you build by genuinely caring about people, over time.

Coby joined a civic organization because someone told him it would be good for his business. He showed up, introduced himself, handed out cards, and waited. Months passed. Nothing materialized. He started wondering whether the whole thing was a waste of time.

Then something shifted. He stopped calculating what the organization owed him and started genuinely engaging with its mission. He volunteered for unglamorous tasks. He stayed to help clean up. He remembered what people told him and followed up the next time he saw them. He was no longer networking. He was participating.

Three years later, someone he had built a genuine friendship with mentioned his name to a friend who needed exactly what Coby did. That friend became a client. Then another. Then referrals from referrals. Over time, that community became one of the most significant sources of opportunity in his professional life. It wasn't because he worked the room, but because he became a trusted, genuine member of it. That is what real relational networking looks like. And it is available to you right now.

The lesson Coby's story carries is not just that patience pays off. It is that the entire orientation has to change. Most students who are thinking about networking are thinking about extracting value from relationships. They are calculating: who can help me? Who has what I need?

What do I gain from this? That orientation is visible to experienced people, and it closes doors.

The professionals in my research who had built the strongest, most productive networks were thinking about something entirely different. They were thinking: what can I contribute? What does this community need? How can I add genuine value to the people around me? That orientation is also visible , and it opens doors in ways that no amount of strategic name-dropping ever could.

Here is the practical implication of the Coby story for where you are right now. You are already a member of communities, your school, your neighborhood, your family's faith community, your team, your club. In every one of those communities, you are already building a reputation, whether you are thinking about it or not. The question is whether the reputation you are building is the one you want.

In every community you belong to, ask yourself: am I here to contribute or to extract? Am I showing up consistently or only when it seems useful? Am I treating the people around me as ends in themselves or as potential means to my own ends? Am I building the kind of reputation that makes people genuinely glad I am here? Those questions, answered honestly and consistently, point toward the posture that builds real social capital.

Start with one community, the one you care about most or spend the most time in. Make a genuine commitment: for the next three months, I will show up every time, I will take on at least one responsibility nobody else wants, I will genuinely care about the people here and demonstrate that care in small, consistent ways. Do that for three months and notice what has changed in how people relate to you. The shift is often more rapid than students expect.

Three Archetypes: Posers, Amateurs, and Professionals

The Posers

Posers treat relationships like vending machines. They focus intensely on getting into the right rooms and meeting the right people, convinced that one powerful connection will change everything overnight. They invest in relationships that seem likely to produce immediate payoffs and neglect those that do not. The fatal flaw of this approach is not just ethical. It is practical: people detect inauthenticity, and when they detect it, they close their networks to you, politely, subtly, but completely.

The poser is often not fully conscious of what they are doing. They genuinely believe they are networking effectively. But the transaction is visible in their body language, in how quickly their attention moves on when a conversation does not produce an obvious opportunity, in the way their interest in someone seems to evaporate once they have gotten what they came for. People remember how you made them feel, long after they have forgotten what you said.

The Amateurs

Amateurs are trying, which puts them ahead. But their approach is unfocused and inconsistent. They throw energy in multiple directions hoping something sticks. Blair, one of my research subjects, described her approach with a phrase that captures the amateur pattern perfectly: "I am throwing my balls into the air to see what sticks." There is real effort. But there is no trajectory, no sustained direction that would allow the effort to accumulate into something lasting. Unfocused effort, however sincere, rarely builds anything real.

The amateur's problem is not motivation or sincerity. It is strategy. They join groups but do not commit deeply enough to any of them to build real relationships. They make introductions but fail to follow up. They attend events but do not do the slower, less glamorous work of maintaining connections over time. Their networks are wide and shallow when what matters is narrow and deep.

The Professionals

Professionals understand something posers and amateurs don't: the relationship is the thing, not the means to an end. They show up to contribute, not extract. They invest in communities they genuinely care about. They are consistently, reliably present. And over time, because they have built real trust and real credibility, opportunities come to them naturally. You do not need a title or a business card to operate with this mindset. You can choose it right now.

> *"People are watching to see how long you will last. If you last long enough, and continue to show up, you gain exposure and people will notice."* ,
> Frank, business owner

Social Capital: Your Most Valuable Professional Asset

Social capital is the accumulated trust, goodwill, and credibility you build through consistent, genuine engagement with the people and communities around you. Think of it as a bank account. Every time you show up when you said you would, follow through on a commitment, contribute genuinely to a group, or treat someone with real care and respect, you make a deposit. Every time you fail to follow through, take more than you give, or behave in a way that makes people trust you less, you make a withdrawal. The cumulative balance of those deposits and withdrawals is your reputation.

Social capital accrues slowly and spends quickly. Building a strong reputation takes years of consistent, genuine deposits. A single significant betrayal of trust can spend years of accumulated capital in an instant. This is why character (how you behave when there is nothing obvious to gain, when nobody is watching, when being honest is inconvenient) is not separate from networking. Character is the foundation of all social capital. Without it, everything else is a facade.

The encouraging thing for you is that social capital starts accumulating from day one. Right now, in the communities you already belong to, through the relationships you already have. The deposits you make today will compound over years into something genuinely powerful.

Here is something that often surprises students: many of the most powerful professional relationships in a person's adult life trace back to high school. The classmate who sat next to you in chemistry class, who you helped study for the final, who you stayed in touch with because you genuinely liked them. Ten years later they are a hiring manager, an investor, a potential collaborator. The relationships you build before anyone has anything obvious to offer are often the deepest and most durable of your entire life. Start making deposits now.

One important nuance about social capital: it cannot be manufactured. You cannot fake your way to a strong reputation. People are remarkably good at detecting inauthenticity, and the attempt to manufacture social capital without doing the genuine work almost always accelerates reputational damage rather than building it.

The only path to a strong reputation is through genuine behavior, consistently repeated over time.

This is actually encouraging news, even if it sounds demanding. It means that the playing field for reputation is genuinely level. You do not need special advantages, special connections, or special resources to start building social capital. You just need to show up consistently, do what you say, care genuinely about the people around you, and contribute honestly to whatever communities you belong to. Start that practice today, and the compounding begins immediately.

There is a practical exercise worth doing. Make a list of the five people whose professional respect you would most want to earn (not celebrities or famous figures), but real people in your actual life or community. Now ask honestly: if each of them thought carefully about you today, based on everything they have observed, what impression would they have? Are you making the deposits you would need to make to earn their genuine respect? If not, what specifically would you need to change? That gap is your roadmap.

Where to Start Building Relationships

Teachers and Counselors

Teachers chose their profession because they want to invest in young people. Most find it genuinely gratifying when a student shows real intellectual curiosity and follows through on advice. A teacher who knows you well can change your trajectory in ways that a perfect transcript alone cannot. They write recommendations. They make introductions. They tell their networks about students who impressed them. Build these relationships deliberately.

The most effective way to build these relationships is not complicated. Go to your teacher's class prepared. Engage with the material honestly. Ask questions that reveal genuine curiosity. Visit office hours not because you are in trouble, but because you want to learn more. Follow through when they suggest a book, a program, or a next step. These small, consistent actions accumulate into a reputation as a student worth investing in.

Classmates

The people in class next to you right now are your future colleagues, collaborators, clients, and references. The relationships you build before anyone has titles or obvious resources to offer are often the deepest and most durable of your professional life. Treat the people around you with the care and intentionality you would want them to show you.

Be the person who helps. Not in a way that enables intellectual dishonesty, but genuinely. For example, studying together, sharing notes, encouraging someone who is struggling. The students who are known for being generous with their time and knowledge build the kind of reputation that follows them far beyond graduation.

Community Organizations

Clubs, volunteer groups, faith communities, sports teams, civic organizations. These are living relationship ecosystems. Do not spread yourself across too many. Join one or two you genuinely care about and invest deeply in them. Show up every time. Take on responsibility. Do the unglamorous work. The relationships built through sustained, genuine involvement are worth far more than a dozen superficial connections made at a networking event.

The key word is sustained. Anyone can show up to one meeting and make a decent impression. What distinguishes the people who build real relationships in organizations is consistency over time. Showing up when it is inconvenient. Completing tasks even when no one is checking. Bringing genuine energy to work that is unglamorous. This is how you go from being someone people recognize to being someone people trust.

Local Professionals and Businesses

If there is a field you are interested in, reach out to someone working in it. This is more accessible than most students imagine. Most professionals, contacted respectfully and specifically by a curious young person who has done their homework, will respond. A single honest conversation with someone doing the work you want to do is worth more than hours of research. Ask for it.

THINK ABOUT IT

Avery, one of the most successful business builders I interviewed, built much of her professional network by being consistently, authentically present wherever she went. She wore her company name on her clothing to her son's games, to the grocery store, to community events. She was not pushy. She was just genuinely engaged with the people around her. Over years, that authentic presence built a business. You can do the same with your personal brand right now, starting with the communities you already belong to.

The Art of Following Through

There is one relationship skill that matters more than almost any other, and that most people are genuinely poor at: following through on what they said they would do.

Following through means responding to the email you committed to responding to. Showing up to the meeting you said you would attend. Reporting back to the mentor who gave you advice. This sounds elementary. And yet it is remarkably, astonishingly rare. Every time you follow through on a commitment , especially a small one, especially an inconvenient one , you make a deposit in your social capital account. Every time you fail, you make a withdrawal. The cumulative effect of these small actions, over months and years, is a reputation that either opens doors or closes them.

Start building the habit of follow-through now, in the smallest interactions, at the lowest possible stakes. The person who follows through consistently develops one of the rarest and most valuable professional qualities that exists.

A practical system: when you make a commitment, write it down immediately, not mentally, but physically. A small notebook, a note in your phone, whatever you will actually check. Review it daily. Do not let commitments fall through the cracks simply because you got busy. The people with the strongest reputations for reliability are almost never the people with the most time. They are the people with the best systems for honoring the commitments they make.

There is a deeper truth beneath the practical advice about follow-through: every time you honor a commitment, you are training yourself to be a certain kind of person. And every time you let one slide, you are training yourself to be a different kind of person. The habits of reliability or unreliability, built in the small moments when nobody is watching and the stakes are low, become the character that shows up in the big moments when everything is at stake.

This is why the habit matters more than any individual instance of follow-through. Nobody expects perfection. Life is genuinely unpredictable, and there will be commitments you genuinely cannot keep. What distinguishes the highly reliable person from the unreliable one is not a perfect record. It is a consistent pattern and a genuine response when the pattern breaks: honest acknowledgment, genuine apology, and immediate action to repair. The person who cannot always keep every commitment but who, when they fail, addresses it immediately and genuinely, builds a reputation for reliability almost as strong as the person who never misses. What destroys reputations is not individual failures but the pattern of ignoring them.

Social Media and Your Relational Reputation

Social media is deeply woven into how your generation builds and maintains reputation. The same dynamics that govern in-person relationships govern online ones: authenticity builds trust, inauthenticity erodes it, consistency creates a reliable picture of who you are.

What is different online is scale and permanence. Before a college admissions officer interviews you, they may look at your social media. Before a potential employer brings you in, they may Google you. This is not a reason to build an impersonal, sanitized online presence. It is a reason to be intentional. Build something you would be proud to have anyone see.

Social media can also be a genuine relationship-building tool if used intentionally. Following and engaging with people working in fields you care about, sharing work you are genuinely proud of, commenting thoughtfully on conversations that matter to you, these actions, done consistently over time, build a presence that attracts the right kind of attention and creates entry points for real relationships. Used this way, social media is not a distraction from relationship-building. It is an extension of it.

A word about the specific challenge social media poses for reputation management. The permanence of digital content means that things posted thoughtlessly at fourteen are potentially still accessible at twenty-four, when you are interviewing for your first professional position. The solution is not to disappear from social media, in many professional contexts, having no digital presence is itself a flag, but to be genuinely intentional about what you put into the permanent digital record.

One useful heuristic: before posting anything, ask yourself whether you would be comfortable if the person you most respect saw this. Not as a way to sanitize your online presence into something generic and impersonal, but as a way to apply the same intentionality online that you would in person. The goal is not a flawless public persona. It is a genuine, consistent, considered one.

In Practice: Building Your Relational Foundation

Relationship-building is not a project with a start date and an end date. It is a practice, a set of habits exercised consistently over time. Here are the habits most worth building right now:

- The Follow-Through Habit: every time you say you will do something, write it down and do it. Start a simple tracker, a note in your phone, a small notebook. Every follow-through is a deposit. Build the streak.
- The Genuine Interest Habit: once a week, reach out to someone in your network with no agenda. Not to ask for anything. To share something interesting, to check in, to acknowledge something they did or said that mattered to you. This habit alone, sustained over years, builds extraordinary social capital.
- The Investment Habit: every week, show up to at least one community you belong to with genuine intent to contribute. Not to be seen. To add something real.
- The Gratitude Habit: once a week, send a specific note of thanks to someone who has done something valuable for you. Not a generic thanks, but a specific one that shows you understood what they gave you. This habit transforms the quality of your relationships faster than almost anything else.

These four habits, practiced weekly for a year, will build a relational foundation that most adults spend decades wishing they had built earlier. They require perhaps thirty minutes per week. The return on that investment, compounded over years, is extraordinary.

The Relational Audit

Once a month, do a ten-minute relational audit. Look at the five people you have spent the most time with this month. Are they lifting you toward who you want to become? Look at the commitments you made this month. Did you honor them? Look at the communities you belong to. Are you a genuine contributor or just a presence? Look at your digital presence. Is it telling the story you want told?

The audit is not about judgment. It is about clarity. The gap between the relational life you are building and the one you want to build is only visible when you look clearly and honestly at both. The audit makes the gap visible so you can close it.

✎ **REFLECTION, THINK, WRITE, ACT**

5. *Name three relationships you want to invest more deeply in. For each one, write one specific thing you will do in the next two weeks.*

6. *Think about the last time you failed to follow through on a commitment. What was the real reason? What habit do you need to build?*

7. *Is there a community organization you have been on the edge of committing to? What is actually holding you back?*

8. *Review your social media presence honestly. If a mentor or potential employer saw it today, what would they think? Is that the story you want told?*

CHAPTER 3

Finding Your Mentor

The right mentor doesn't just give you advice. They see who you can become before you can see it yourself.

Marcus and Dempsey were in the same professional field. Comparable credentials. Comparable work ethic. But when I interviewed them, they were in dramatically different places.

Marcus was thriving. When I asked him what had made the biggest difference, his answer was immediate: his mentor. He named the person, described how they met, and walked me through the specific ways that relationship had changed his trajectory. His mentor taught him the unwritten rules of his industry, made introductions that opened doors he could not have accessed alone, and told him hard truths nobody else was willing to say. Marcus had not done it alone.

Dempsey was struggling. He was intelligent, hardworking, committed. When I asked about his support system, he described family and community, people who loved and encouraged him. But when I pressed him about whether he had someone with specific professional knowledge who was teaching him the inside game, the answer was no. He was navigating a complex professional landscape largely alone, relying on people who cared deeply about him but lacked the specific knowledge to help him grow. Same field. One thriving. One struggling. One of the clearest explanations was the presence or absence of real mentorship.

The Marcus and Dempsey contrast showed up, in different forms, across dozens of interviews. It was one of the most consistent findings in the entire research. The people who had found and cultivated genuine mentoring relationships were dramatically better positioned than those who had not, not because of luck or because mentors handed them opportunities, but because real mentorship accelerated the development of every other intangible. A great mentor helps you build relationships. They help clarify your vision. They teach you how to present yourself. They hold you accountable to your goals. In this sense, mentorship is the force multiplier of all the other intangibles.

What Real Mentorship Actually Is

A mentor is not a cheerleader. A mentor is someone who has traveled some version of the road you are trying to travel and is willing to be honest with you about what it actually requires. The core of what they do is not to make you feel good. It is to help you grow. And growth requires honest feedback, which often means things that are genuinely uncomfortable.

Joel, one of the successful professionals I interviewed, described real mentorship with unusual clarity. A mentor, he said, teaches you the ropes, not just the formal curriculum, but the real curriculum. They notice when you are wearing the wrong thing to a meeting and say so. They go beyond the surface of the professional relationship and take genuine interest in your trajectory, your reputation, your potential. They call you when they think you need to hear something, not just when you reach out.

A mentor is also different from a sponsor, an advisor, or a friend. A sponsor advocates for you in rooms you are not in, a powerful relationship but one that typically takes years to develop. An advisor gives you information on request. A friend provides emotional support. A mentor provides something different from all of these: sustained, honest investment in your development as a whole person, grounded in specific knowledge of the road you are trying to travel.

> *"A true mentor takes a real interest in you. They teach you the ropes, the best way to say things, the best way to do things. They go beyond what you do every day."* , Joel, 20-year business veteran

Nine Things a Great Mentor Does

- Keeps you accountable to the specific goals and commitments you have made. When you drift, they notice and say something.
- Maintains consistent, proactive communication. They do not wait for a crisis to check in.
- Nurtures your development as a whole person, not just your performance on specific tasks.
- Takes real, sustained interest in your specific situation. They remember what you told them last time.
- Shows you the unwritten rules, the norms that are never formally documented but that everyone who has been around long enough knows.
- Models the behavior and standards required to succeed through their own conduct.
- Pulls you through your mistakes rather than abandoning you. They help you understand what happened and move forward.
- Provides information and opens doors proactively, without waiting for you to know the right questions to ask.

- Intervenes on your behalf with credibility when you need someone to go to bat for you.

The Unwritten Curriculum

One of the most valuable things a mentor provides is access to what I call the unwritten curriculum, the norms, expectations, and insider knowledge that are never formally documented but that everyone who has been in a field long enough has absorbed. Every industry, every organization, every professional context has one. The unwritten curriculum tells you how people actually get ahead in this specific environment, what mistakes are unrecoverable and which are tolerable, who the informal power brokers are and how they like to be approached, what signals competence versus what merely signals effort.

Without a mentor, the only way to learn the unwritten curriculum is through experience, which means paying for it through mistakes. A mentor who teaches it to you proactively is saving you years of costly, unnecessary trial and error. This is one of the most concrete and measurable values of mentorship, and it is one that students, who often feel like mentors are only valuable later in a career, consistently underestimate.

Think about any environment you want to enter: a college program, a professional field, a type of organization. There is an unwritten curriculum there. Things that the people who thrive know and follow without thinking about them, that the people who struggle violate without knowing they exist. A mentor who has been in that environment can show you that curriculum before you arrive. That advance knowledge is worth more than almost anything you can learn in a classroom.

I want to give you a concrete example of the unwritten curriculum in action. Terrence, one of the successful professionals I interviewed, described walking into his first major client meeting wearing a suit that was technically appropriate but clearly off in some way he could not identify. His mentor, who had attended the meeting with him, pulled him aside afterward and told him: the cut is wrong for this client base. These are people who favor a more casual professional aesthetic. You are going to want to shift your wardrobe slightly if you want to work consistently with this type of client.

That was a piece of information Terrence could not have gotten from any formal training. He would have had to learn it through repeated experience, through noticing patterns over months, through getting the subtle feedback that nobody delivers directly, through trial and error at real professional cost. His mentor gave him the insight in five minutes. That is the unwritten curriculum. And it applies to every dimension of professional life: how to communicate in writing, how to handle disagreement in meetings, how to navigate organizational politics, what counts as initiative versus overstepping, how to deliver bad news. Every field has its specific version of this knowledge, and a mentor who is willing to share it proactively is one of the most powerful professional assets you can have.

Support vs. Mentorship: A Critical Distinction

Emotional support, the love, encouragement, and unconditional belief your family and close friends give you, is genuinely important. People with strong emotional support systems are more resilient, more willing to take healthy risks, more able to recover from setbacks. Do not minimize it.

But emotional support is not mentorship. Rigby, one of the struggling professionals I interviewed, had a strong support system, family who loved him, friends who encouraged him. But when I asked whether he had someone with specific professional knowledge who could help him understand why his approach was not working, the answer was no. His supporters were wonderful people. But wonderful people who lack specific knowledge in your field cannot help you grow professionally, no matter how much they love you. Seek both. Know the difference.

The confusion between support and mentorship is one of the most consequential and underappreciated gaps in how young people think about their development. You can be surrounded by people who believe in you completely, parents, friends, community members, and still be navigating the actual professional landscape alone, without access to the specific knowledge and honest feedback that would help you grow. Both are necessary. Neither substitutes for the other.

REAL TALK

Ian found his mentor almost entirely by accident. He called an office for information, and the person who answered was warm and genuinely helpful. They struck up a conversation. Ian followed up. Over time, the relationship grew into one of the most important of Ian's professional life. He did not find his mentor through a program or a strategic networking move. He found him by paying attention to people who showed up willing to help, and by cultivating the relationship with genuine care and consistency. Mentors do not always arrive with labels.

How to Find a Mentor in High School

The most common barrier students face in finding mentors is not a scarcity of willing adults. It is an unwillingness to ask. Most students who do not have mentors have not asked anyone to serve in that role. They are waiting to be discovered, waiting for a program to formalize the relationship, waiting until they feel ready. None of these strategies work.

There is a specific kind of courage required to ask for mentorship, and it is worth naming directly. The ask makes you vulnerable. It declares that you want to become better than you currently are, which requires acknowledging that you are not yet where you want to be. It positions you as someone who needs guidance, which feels uncomfortable for students who have been praised primarily for what they already know. And it risks rejection, the person you ask might say no, or might not have time, or might not be the right fit.

All of those discomforts are real. None of them are reasons not to ask. The mentor you never ask for is one hundred percent unavailable. The mentor you ask for might say yes, and might change your trajectory. The asymmetry of that calculation is overwhelming. Ask. The worst outcome is a no that costs you nothing. The best outcome is a relationship that changes your life.

In Practice: Your Mentor Search This Month

The difference between students who have mentors and those who do not is almost entirely the difference between those who ask and those who wait. Here is a four-step process for finding your first mentor, or deepening an existing mentoring relationship, within the next thirty days.

9. Identify three adults in your life or community who have knowledge or experience directly relevant to where you want to go. Not people who are generally wise and supportive, people with specific professional experience in an area you care about. Write their names down.
10. Research each of them. If they have a professional profile, read it. If they have work or writing you can find, engage with it. The goal is to walk into any conversation with them already knowing something specific about their background and having a genuine question grounded in that knowledge.
11. Reach out to your first choice with a specific, bounded request. The message should be brief, respectful, specific, and clearly bounded in time: "I am a high school student with a genuine interest in [field]. I have done some reading on your work and would be incredibly grateful for even twenty minutes of your perspective on [specific question]. Would you be willing to connect at some point this month?"
12. After any conversation, send a specific thanks within twenty-four hours. Reference something from the conversation. If they gave you advice, take it and report back. Every follow-through deepens the relationship.

If the first person says no, reach out to the second. If the second says no, reach out to the third. Most will say yes. People who have built something real generally want to share what they learned. They are waiting for someone to ask with genuine curiosity and appropriate respect.

THINK ABOUT IT

Think about the most impressive professional in your orbit, someone who is further along the path you want to take and clearly doing something real. Have you ever told them you admire what they have built and that you would like to learn from their experience? If the answer is no, there is your assignment. Do not wait for a formal mentorship program or a perfectly crafted request. Reach out with genuine curiosity and honest respect. The conversation you are afraid to start is the one most likely to change your trajectory.

When you do ask, be specific and respectful of the person's time. Not: "Would you be my mentor?", which is vague, open-ended, and implicitly asks for an indefinite commitment. Instead: "I am trying to figure out how to get from where I am to where I want to be in this field, and I would be incredibly grateful for even thirty minutes of your perspective. Would you be willing to meet with me once to share your experience?" That request is specific, bounded, and easy to say yes to. From a good conversation, ongoing relationships develop naturally. Start with one conversation.

13. Start with adults already in your life. Teachers, coaches, counselors, family friends, community leaders. Who has knowledge relevant to where you want to go?
14. Identify people working in fields that interest you. Look locally first, then more broadly. LinkedIn, used thoughtfully, can be remarkably effective.
15. Show genuine interest before asking for anything. Read their work, attend events they are involved in, ask specific questions that reveal you have done your homework.

16. Make specific, time-bounded requests. Not "Be my mentor", but "Would you be willing to spend thirty minutes with me this month to talk about your path into this field?"
17. Follow through on absolutely everything. Take advice and report back. Make every introduction count. Every instance of follow-through deepens the relationship.
18. Be patient. Mentoring relationships develop over months and years. Show up consistently, ask good questions, do what you say you will do.

One additional strategy worth emphasizing: look for people who are already generous with their time and knowledge. Some people are natural teachers who are genuinely energized by helping younger people develop. These are the people most likely to invest in you if you approach them thoughtfully. Pay attention to who in your community has a reputation for being genuinely helpful and investing in others, they are your best candidates.

Being a Mentee Worth Investing In

The quality of your engagement determines how deeply a mentor will invest. The most investable mentees bring:

- Reliability: doing what they say, when they say, without needing to be chased.
- Genuine curiosity: asking real questions to learn, not to impress.
- Humility: receiving hard feedback without becoming defensive.
- Transparency: being honest about what is going well and what is not.
- Gratitude: acknowledging the relationship's value genuinely.

- Initiative: bringing their own energy and questions rather than waiting to be led.

The mentee who shows up prepared, listens carefully, takes advice seriously, and reports back on what they did with it is giving their mentor the most valuable thing a mentor can receive: evidence that the investment is working. Mentors are human beings with limited time. They will naturally invest more in the mentees who make that investment worthwhile. Be the mentee that makes it obvious.

✎ **REFLECTION, THINK, WRITE, ACT**

19. *Who in your life has knowledge or experience genuinely relevant to where you want to go? Have you ever asked them directly to share it?*

20. *Think of one teacher, coach, or community adult you admire. What one specific, time-bounded request could you make of them in the next two weeks?*

21. *Think of a time you received honest, uncomfortable feedback. What did you do with it? What does your response say about you as a potential mentee?*

22. *What one type of specific knowledge do you most lack and most need? Who might be able to help you get it?*

CHAPTER 4

How You Show Up

You are communicating something before you say a single word. The question is whether you are communicating what you intend.

Before you open your mouth in any room that matters, impressions are already forming. People are deciding, below the level of conscious thought, what kind of person you are, based on visible, immediate information: how you carry yourself, how you are dressed, whether your eyes are engaged or distracted, whether your posture says I am here and I am paying attention or I would rather be somewhere else.

This is not theory. It is a well-documented feature of human social cognition. We make rapid assessments of people we encounter, and those assessments happen in the first few seconds of meeting someone and persist stubbornly. The judgments people form in those initial moments about your competence, reliability, and trustworthiness are highly durable and highly influential on everything that follows. Understanding this is not an invitation to be inauthentic. It is an invitation to be intentional. You are always sending a message. The only question is whether you have chosen it.

Consider two students applying for the same competitive internship. They have similar GPAs and similar extracurricular involvement. The first student arrives to the interview having researched the organization, dressed professionally, makes eye contact, listens carefully, and asks specific questions that reveal genuine curiosity. The second student arrives in casual clothes, checks their phone twice during the interview, and gives vague answers that suggest they did not prepare much. The second student may be equally intelligent and equally capable. But the first student has communicated something the second has not: that they take this seriously, that they respect the people they are meeting with, and that they know how to show up.

Why Image Is Strategic, Not Shallow

Caring about how you present yourself is not vanity. It is strategy. Your image is the wrapper for your substance. A great gift in a careless wrapper sends a confusing message about how much the giver valued it. Your character, your intelligence, your potential, these are your substance. Your image is the wrapper that either gives those things the chance to be recognized or creates a first impression people have to work hard to overcome.

> *"The impression we make on others by the way we look is a reality of life. People react to these impressions in an instinctive, involuntary way. These impressions are long-lasting and amazingly consistent."*

Being intentional about your image does not mean being someone you are not. It means being the fullest, most intentional version of who you actually are. The student who shows up to an important interview in clothes they feel confident in, having prepared thoughtfully, is not pretending to be someone else. They are showing up as their most capable self. That is what intentional self-presentation means.

Dressing for the Room You Want to Enter

One of the most actionable pieces of advice in this chapter: dress for the room you want to be in, not just the room you are currently in. Research what is appropriate for the specific contexts that matter to you and show up in a way that communicates you took those contexts seriously.

Shawnte, a boutique owner in a high-end neighborhood, noticed one day that a regular customer glanced at her unmanicured feet with an expression that said everything. She immediately made grooming a non-negotiable part of her professional routine. Not because vanity demanded it, but because she understood that in her environment, personal presentation was part of the product. Steve, a painting contractor, drove a 535 BMW to his first construction job site. A job site where the culture is to drive American cars. The supervisor told him bluntly to park it somewhere else. Was it fair? Debatable. Did acting on it change his business? Absolutely. The lesson from both: details of presentation communicate things, and in environments that matter to you, those details are being noticed.

The challenge for students is that different contexts have very different norms, and navigating between them requires genuine contextual intelligence. What is appropriate for a job interview at a law firm is different from what is appropriate for an internship at a tech startup. What is appropriate for a college admissions office visit is different from what is appropriate for a college campus tour. The skill is not dressing the same way in every situation. It is reading the room accurately and showing up in a way that respects the norms of the specific context.

The best strategy: research in advance. Look at the website and social media of any organization you are visiting. Notice how people dress in photos. If you are not sure, it is almost always better to err slightly on the side of more formal. You can almost always loosen the impression you make. It is much harder to recover from an impression of carelessness.

Body Language, Presence, and Eye Contact

How you show up goes far beyond what you wear. Eye contact says: I see you, I am listening, I am present. Practice looking at people when they are speaking to you with genuine, sustained attention. It is more powerful than most people realize.

Posture communicates energy and engagement before you say anything. Genuine presence, phone completely away, attention fully engaged, has become remarkably rare. The person who is genuinely present stands out with startling clarity. It costs nothing. Its impact is significant.

The handshake, yes, this still matters in professional contexts, communicates a great deal. Firm, confident, appropriate duration, accompanied by eye contact and a genuine smile. Practice it. The first physical interaction with someone new sets a tone that is surprisingly durable.

Active listening is perhaps the most underestimated presence skill. Most people, in most conversations, are primarily waiting for their turn to speak rather than genuinely attending to what the other person is saying. The person who truly listens, who asks follow-up questions that reveal they understood and were paying attention, who remembers details and references them later, creates a completely different impression from the person who nods politely while their mind is elsewhere.

Genuine listening is a form of generosity that people feel deeply and remember.

There is a complementary skill to genuine listening that is worth developing alongside it: the ability to ask good questions. A good question in a professional context is one that reveals you were genuinely listening and thinking, that you synthesized something from what was said and built on it. Bad questions are those that could have been answered by reading the organization's website, or that ask for information you should already have, or that are primarily designed to make you look smart rather than to gather genuine insight.

Practice asking the kind of question that says: I was genuinely here, I processed what you said, and I want to go deeper. That kind of question is one of the clearest signals of intellectual engagement available. It is also, frankly, much rarer than it should be. The person who asks genuinely good questions stands out in almost every professional context, not because they are showing off, but because genuine curiosity and engagement are so obviously present in what they ask.

THINK ABOUT IT

Before your next meaningful professional interaction, an informational interview, a mentor meeting, a college visit, prepare three to five questions in advance. Not generic questions, but specific ones based on real research into the person or organization you are meeting. Ask about something specific on their website. Reference something they have written or said publicly. Show that you did the work. The quality of your preparation is visible before you say anything, and it makes every subsequent impression significantly stronger.

Your Digital Presence

Your first impression is often made online before you and the other person are ever in the same room. Before a college admissions officer reads your application, they may look at your social media. Before a potential employer interviews you, they may Google you. Your digital presence is a portfolio, an ongoing record of who you are and what you choose to be publicly associated with. The question to ask is not whether you have done anything technically wrong. The question is whether what is publicly visible about you tells the story you actually want told.

Audit your presence. Google yourself. Look at every public-facing profile through the eyes of someone who does not know you. What does it say about your character, your interests, your maturity? Does it reflect the person you want to be known as? If not, make changes, both by removing things that do not serve you and by building things that do.

LinkedIn is worth setting up now, even if you are in high school. A thoughtful, professional profile that reflects your genuine interests, experiences, and goals signals seriousness and maturity in ways that count. It also allows you to connect with and engage with professionals in fields you care about before you need anything from them. That is the ideal time to build those connections.

The Space You Create

Once you are in contexts with any kind of workspace or professional environment, that space tells a story. Organized, intentional materials communicate something different than disarray. A prompt follow-up email communicates something different than silence. Every touchpoint is an opportunity to reinforce or undermine the impression you are making. Be intentional about what all of those data points add up to.

The follow-up note is worth specific attention. After a meaningful professional interaction, an informational interview, a meeting with a mentor, a job interview, send a brief, specific, genuine note of thanks within twenty-four hours. Reference something specific from the conversation to demonstrate that you were genuinely present and listening. This simple action is so rare that it reliably makes an impression. Most people never do it. The ones who do stand out immediately.

In Practice: Your Presence Audit

Here is a practical self-assessment for how you currently show up. Rate yourself honestly, from one to five, on each of the following dimensions. Not how you would like to show up, how you actually do, right now, in the contexts that matter to you.

- Physical appearance: Does my clothing and grooming communicate that I take myself and my context seriously? (1 = rarely, 5 = consistently)
- Eye contact and active listening: Do I give my full attention to the people I am with, or do I get distracted? (1 = rarely, 5 = consistently)
- Digital presence: Does my public online presence reflect the person I want to be known as? (1 = not at all, 5 = completely)
- Follow-up communication: Do I send genuine, timely follow-up after meaningful professional interactions? (1 = never, 5 = always)
- Phone presence: When I am with people who deserve my full attention, is my phone put away? (1 = rarely, 5 = consistently)

Add up your scores. A 20 or above is genuinely strong presence. Below 15 suggests significant room to improve. Whatever your score, identify the single lowest-rated item and make that your focus for the next thirty days. Small, specific improvements, consistently applied, move the needle faster than trying to improve everything at once.

The Digital Audit

Set aside thirty minutes and do the following: Google yourself. Look at every piece of public information available about you. Look at every public social media profile. Now ask: if the person I most want to impress professionally saw all of this today, what would they think? Write your honest answer below, then write one specific thing you will change this week.

What I will change this week:

✎ **REFLECTION, THINK, WRITE, ACT**

23. *If someone who had never met you looked at your complete digital presence today, what would they think? What would you change?*

24. *Think of a specific upcoming situation where how you show up will matter. What will you do to prepare your image, your body language, and your presence?*

25. *What is one aspect of how you currently present yourself that does not reflect who you want to be? What one specific change can you make this week?*

26. *When was the last time you were fully, genuinely present in a conversation, phone away, attention fully engaged? How did it feel compared to a normal interaction?*

CHAPTER 5

Your Vision: Where Are You Going?

"Where there is no vision, the people perish.", Proverbs 29:18

Luke was one of the struggling professionals in my research. Hardworking, committed, years in the field. When I asked what had held him back, he said: "A vision helps make you stand out. It guides your connection with organizations and the people within them." He was describing, in retrospect, what he had lacked. He had been busy without direction. And business without direction, no matter how energetic and sincere, is not the same as progress.

Vision is not a plan. Plans change and are supposed to change, they adapt as circumstances do. A vision is something deeper: the image of who you want to become and the life you want to live. It is the destination, not the route. When the route changes, as it always does, the destination remains. That stability is what makes vision so powerful.

The difference between a plan and a vision is the difference between a map and a compass. A map tells you specific roads to take. When those roads are closed, a map becomes useless. A compass tells you which direction is north. No matter what obstacles you encounter, no matter how many detours you take, you can always reorient toward north. Vision is your compass. The routes you take to follow it will change many times over the course of a life. The direction it points does not.

You Don't Need Certainty to Start

The most common objection I hear from students: I don't know what I want yet. How can I have a vision? You do not need a fixed, permanent, perfectly detailed picture of your entire future. That kind of premature certainty can actually limit you, making you unwilling to follow unexpected opportunities that turn out to be the most important ones. What you need is a direction. A general orientation toward who you want to become, what impact you want to have, and what values you want to live by. Even a rough, provisional, imperfect direction is enormously more powerful than none at all.

Jordan, a successful business builder I interviewed, declared his goals publicly, not because he was certain they were right, but because declaring a direction made it real and created productive accountability. You can do the same. Start with one question: who do I want to become? Not what do I want to do. Not what do I want to have. Who do I want to be? The answer to that question is the seed of a vision that can guide everything else.

Many students confuse having a vision with having a career answer. They are not the same thing. Your vision is a picture of who you are becoming as a person, your values, your character, the kind of impact you want to have, the quality of relationships you want to build. A career is one expression of that vision. The vision comes first; the career is downstream of it. Students who try to choose a career without a vision are choosing a vehicle without knowing where they are going.

What Vision Does for You

- Organizes your decisions. When you know where you are going, evaluating choices becomes dramatically clearer. Does this move me toward my destination or away from it?

- Provides resilience. When things go wrong, and they will, a vision gives you a reason to keep going. People without one often treat a serious setback as a reason to stop. People with one treat it as an obstacle to route around.
- Attracts the right people. Mentors, collaborators, and supporters are drawn to people who have a clear sense of direction. A vision signals seriousness and intentionality.
- Filters out the noise. Without a vision, every distraction seems as valid as every opportunity. With one, you can say no clearly and confidently to things that do not serve your direction.
- Keeps you honest. A vision is a standard you can measure yourself against. It makes the gap between where you are and where you want to be visible, sometimes uncomfortable and always necessary.

The filtering function of vision is particularly valuable for students, because high school presents an almost overwhelming number of commitments competing for your attention. Which clubs to join. Which opportunities to pursue. How to spend your evenings and weekends. Without a vision, every option seems equally valid and the result is often paralysis or scattered, unfocused effort. With a vision, evaluation becomes straightforward: does this serve who I am becoming? If yes, invest. If no, decline gracefully and without guilt.

There is one more function of vision that deserves its own attention: it makes you significantly more attractive to mentors and collaborators. People who have a clear sense of direction, who can articulate where they are going and why, signal something important: that investing in them is likely to produce results. Mentors are human beings with limited time. They naturally gravitate toward mentees who will use what they offer effectively. A student with a vision makes that investment feel worthwhile in a way that a student without one simply cannot.

This dynamic extends beyond mentors. Teammates, collaborators, teachers, community leaders, everyone who could invest in your development makes implicit judgments about whether that investment is likely to be worthwhile. Clarity of vision does not have to be perfect to make this impression. It just has to be genuine. The student who says, honestly and specifically, what they are trying to build and why they care about it makes a fundamentally different impression than the student who shrugs and says they are not sure yet.

Practice articulating your vision out loud. Find a trusted adult or friend and say it to them. Notice where it gets vague or uncomfortable, those are the areas where more honest thinking is needed. The vision that you can articulate clearly, to another person, in two or three sentences, is the one that will actually guide your decisions. The one that lives only in your head, fuzzy and unexamined, is mostly decoration.

In Practice: Building Your Vision This Month

Here is a structured four-session process for developing a genuine personal vision. Each session takes about thirty minutes. Do them in different environments, somewhere quiet, somewhere you find energizing, somewhere that helps you think. Give yourself a week between sessions to sit with what you wrote.

Session 1: Values Clarification

Look at the values list in Chapter 5. Choose your top ten. Then narrow to your top five. Then narrow to your top three. For each of your top three, write two or three sentences describing what this value means to you specifically, not the dictionary definition, but what it means in your actual life, with real examples. Then ask: in the last month, how consistently did my actual choices reflect these values? Be honest.

Session 2: The Five-Year Picture

Write continuously for twenty minutes answering this question: Five years from now, what does a genuinely good day look like for me? Where am I? What am I working on? Who is around me? How do I feel when I wake up? What have I built? Do not edit. Do not worry about whether it sounds impressive or realistic. Just write honestly. After twenty minutes, read back through and circle the words that feel most true.

Session 3: The Gap and the First Step

Look at what you wrote in Session 2. Now look at your current reality. Describe the gap honestly. What is the single most significant difference between where you are now and the person you described in Session 2? Then identify the single most important first step toward closing that gap. Not a five-year plan. One specific first step you can take in the next thirty days.

Session 4: Your Vision Statement

Using everything from the first three sessions, write two or three sentences that constitute your personal vision statement. Include: who you want to become, what impact you want to have, and what values will guide you. Then share it with one person you trust and ask them to tell you if it sounds like you, genuinely, honestly, like the person they know.

Date this vision statement and keep it somewhere you will see it regularly. Review it in six months. Notice what has changed and what has held. The vision that grows with you is the one doing real work.

One useful way to test whether your vision is genuinely yours versus inherited from someone else: notice how you feel when you imagine actually living it. A vision that is genuinely yours produces a specific kind of resonance, a feeling of recognition, of rightness, even if the path to it feels daunting. A vision borrowed from someone else's expectations produces something different: a hollow feeling, or a kind of flatness, or a vague sense that you are describing someone else's life.

The inherited vision is one of the most common and costly traps young people fall into. The student who pursues medicine because their parents expect it, or law because it seems prestigious, or a specific college because it is the one everyone in their social circle aspires to, these students often arrive at their destinations and discover that the destination does not fit. The work of developing a genuine vision is partly the work of separating your own values and aspirations from the overlay of other people's expectations. That work is difficult. It requires honesty and courage. It is also one of the most important things you can do.

A practice worth trying: write a vision statement that you would be embarrassed to share with your parents or your most achievement-oriented peers. Not because embarrassing your parents is the goal, but because the things we would be embarrassed to admit we want are often the things we want most genuinely. The vision you hide is sometimes the truest one. Let it speak.

Building Your Vision Statement

Find quiet time, not five minutes between classes, but a real stretch when you can think without interruption. Work through these questions honestly:

- What kind of person do I want to be known as? Not by title, but by character.
- What impact do I most want to have, on my family, my community, the wider world?
- What does a genuinely fulfilling life look like to me, in my own honest assessment?
- What values do I want to live by regardless of circumstances?

- Where do I want to be in five years? In ten? What does the person living that life look like on a Tuesday morning?

Write your answers. Then distill them into two or three honest, specific sentences. That is your starting vision statement. It will evolve as you grow. The act of committing it to paper is the powerful step.

Two common traps when writing a vision statement. The first is writing what you think you should want rather than what you actually want. If your vision statement sounds like it was written to impress someone else, it will not guide you effectively. Write for an audience of one: the honest version of yourself. The second trap is making the vision so grand and abstract that it provides no practical guidance. "Making the world a better place" is a sentiment, not a vision. Get specific. The more honest and specific your vision, the more work it will do for you.

THINK ABOUT IT

Write a personal mission statement right now. A short paragraph answering: who am I, what do I stand for, what am I working toward, and how do I want to treat the people around me? Keep it honest and specific. Read it in a month. Notice what has changed and what has stayed the same. A mission statement is a living document, it is supposed to evolve with you.

Core Values: The Compass Beneath the Vision

Vision without values is just ambition. And ambition without values will drive you toward success at any cost. Values are the principles guiding your choices when the stakes are high and the right path is not obvious. They are what you hold onto when everything external is shifting.

- Integrity, doing what is right even when it costs you something, especially when nobody is watching
- Growth, always learning, always improving, never settling for stagnation
- Service, using your capabilities to contribute to something beyond yourself
- Courage, acting on what you believe even when it is uncomfortable or risky
- Loyalty, standing by people and principles through difficulty, not just convenience
- Excellence, refusing to do less than your best when it genuinely matters
- Compassion, genuinely caring about the wellbeing of the people around you
- Honesty, telling the truth, particularly when it is inconvenient
- Perseverance, staying with something through difficulty until it yields

Choose your top three or four. Write them down somewhere visible. Let them be the filter through which you evaluate your choices, not just the big decisions, but the small daily ones that do most of the work of shaping who you become.

Values are tested by the small moments, not just the dramatic ones. It is relatively easy to be honest when the cost of honesty is low. It is much harder when honesty will disappoint someone you care about, or when it will cost you something. The person who holds to their values when it is costly, and does so consistently, in small moments as well as large ones, builds a character that becomes one of their most durable assets.

When the Vision Gets Blurry

Having a vision does not mean you will always feel clear and motivated. There will be long stretches when the future feels foggy, when the gap between where you are and where you want to be feels impossibly wide. This is normal. It is not a sign your vision is wrong. It is a sign you are working toward something genuinely difficult. The people who persist through these periods are not those who never doubt. They are those who have something to return to. The habit of regularly returning to your vision statement, revisiting your values, renewing your commitment to your direction, this is one of the most important habits you can build.

There is a practice worth developing: scheduled reflection. Once a month, set aside thirty minutes with your vision statement, your values list, and an honest assessment of the last thirty days. Did your choices reflect your values? Did your investments of time and attention move you toward your vision? What needs to change? This practice, done consistently, keeps your vision alive and your direction clear across the inevitable periods when everything feels uncertain.

✎ **REFLECTION, THINK, WRITE, ACT**

27. *Write a rough first draft of your personal vision statement right now. Two or three sentences. Even incomplete, write something real.*

28. *What are your top three core values? Think of a decision you made in the last month. Did it actually reflect those values?*

29. *Think of a decision you are currently facing. How does your emerging vision help clarify what to do?*

30. *Is there a version of success you are pursuing because someone else wants it for you rather than because you genuinely want it? What would change if you chose based entirely on your own vision?*

CHAPTER 6

Creating Your Edge

The most successful people don't just work harder in one dimension. They invest intentionally across every dimension of their lives.

One morning at a café, a conversation introduced me to a concept called Kāla, a Sanskrit word meaning time. The framework: a genuinely fulfilling, sustainable life is built through deliberate investment across five interdependent dimensions. Neglect any one and the whole system weakens. Invest genuinely in all five and something remarkable happens: the different parts of your life stop competing and start reinforcing each other.

When I held that framework against my research data, I saw it confirmed everywhere. The thriving professionals were not simply working harder. They were living more intentionally across multiple dimensions. The five elements of Kāla are: professional and career growth, personal relationships, spirituality and inner life, personal development and lifelong learning, and civic and community relationships.

What made the Kāla framework so resonant was how precisely it matched the patterns I had found independently in my research. The struggling professionals had not failed at one thing. They had inadvertently neglected one or two dimensions of their lives in ways that eventually weakened everything else. The thriving professionals had not succeeded in one thing. They had built, whether consciously or not, across all five dimensions. The framework gave me language for what I had been observing.

Element One: Professional and Career Growth

For you right now, professional growth means developing your skills and knowledge, taking your education seriously as genuine development rather than credential-earning, and actively exploring what is actually available to you. Most students have a far narrower picture of what professional life can look like than the actual range of possibilities. The most interesting careers, and the ones most relevant to the world you are entering, are often the least visible from where you are standing.

This is an argument for active, open-ended exploration. Shadow someone in a field that intrigues you. Start a project that forces you to develop capabilities you do not currently have. Talk honestly with people who have careers you find interesting about what those careers actually require day-to-day. The student who arrives at their next stage having explored broadly and developed genuine expertise in something they care about has a head start that no credential can manufacture.

Professional growth in high school also means developing the habits that make professional growth possible: the discipline to work consistently, the ability to meet deadlines, the capacity to receive and act on feedback, the willingness to do things you find difficult. These habits, built now at low stakes, are the foundation of everything that comes next.

Element Two: Personal Relationships

The people you spend the most time with will shape who you become more profoundly than almost any other factor in your life. Not through dramatic events, but through the slow, cumulative, largely invisible effect of daily exposure. What you talk about. What you take seriously. What ambitions feel possible versus ridiculous. All of this is shaped by the people closest to you.

Invest deliberately in relationships that lift you up and challenge you to grow. Be honest with yourself about relationships that consistently pull you away from who you want to become. This does not require dramatic confrontations, just clarity about where you are investing your time and attention, and whether that investment is serving the person you want to be.

The quality of your personal relationships is not just important for your happiness. It is important for your resilience. People who have strong, genuine personal relationships recover faster from setbacks, take healthier risks, and make better decisions. The social support that comes from genuine relationships is one of the strongest predictors of both wellbeing and long-term success in the research literature. Invest in it accordingly.

Element Three: Spirituality and Inner Life

Spirituality, in this framework, means grounding. The stable center you return to when everything external is shifting. The answer to the question: when all the external things fall away, who am I and what do I believe? It does not require any specific religious tradition. It requires the deliberate cultivation of whatever anchors you, faith, philosophy, meditation, time in nature, a practice of reflection, and the recognition that your grounding is not separate from your success. It is one of its foundations.

People who are genuinely grounded make better decisions under pressure. They are more resilient when things go wrong. They are less easily manipulated by circumstances or the opinions of others, because they have their own compass. Invest in your inner life as seriously as you invest in your skills.

In practical terms, cultivating your inner life might mean a regular journaling practice, a consistent prayer or meditation routine, regular time in nature, or any other practice that helps you return to what matters when the noise of daily life gets loud. The specific form is less important than the consistency. The goal is a reliable inner compass that you have developed deliberately and can access reliably.

Element Four: Personal Development and Lifelong Learning

The world you are entering changes faster than any previous generation has had to navigate. The specific technical skills most valued today will look substantially different in ten years. Given that reality, the meta-skill most consistently valuable is the capacity for learning itself. People who are genuinely good at learning do not become irrelevant when their industry changes. They simply learn the new thing. That adaptability is a strategic asset more durable than any specific technical skill.

Cultivate this capacity deliberately. Read broadly beyond your area of interest. Take care of your body, because physical health is the infrastructure that makes cognitive performance, emotional regulation, and resilience possible. Develop intellectual curiosity as a daily practice, not an occasional indulgence.

Curiosity is the engine of personal development. The student who is genuinely curious about how things work, about the experiences and ideas of people different from themselves, about fields they know nothing about yet, this student is building an asset that no curriculum can provide. Read books that have nothing to do with school.

Talk to people whose lives look completely different from yours. Seek out experiences that challenge your current understanding of the world. The person who is consistently curious is, almost inevitably, one of the most interesting and insightful people in any room.

There is a habit called deliberate practice that researchers in human performance have identified as the most reliable driver of expertise. Deliberate practice is not just doing something repeatedly. It is doing something with full concentration, with immediate feedback, and with the specific intention of improving on weaknesses rather than reinforcing strengths. The student who reads passively is not developing the same capacity as the one who reads actively, pausing, questioning, connecting ideas, testing understanding.

In Practice: Your Kāla Assessment

Take twenty minutes and honestly assess where you are in each of the five Kāla elements. This is not about judging yourself. It is about seeing clearly so you can invest intentionally.

Professional and Career Growth

What am I currently doing to actively develop my professional knowledge and skills? What is the most significant gap between where I am and where I want to be in this area?

Personal Relationships

Who are the two or three people with the most positive influence on who I am becoming? What is one relationship I am currently neglecting that deserves more investment?

Spirituality and Inner Life

What grounds me when everything external is uncertain? Do I have a consistent practice that maintains my inner stability? What would I need to start or deepen?

Personal Development and Lifelong Learning

What am I currently learning beyond what is required? What is the last book I read entirely by choice? What would I study if there were no grades attached?

Civic and Community

What communities do I genuinely belong to and contribute to? Is there a cause I care about deeply enough to invest significant time in consistently?

Now identify the element with the biggest gap between current investment and desired investment. Write one specific commitment for how you will invest in it differently this month. Make it concrete, time-bound, and realistic. Then do it.

My commitment:

By when:

How I will know I did it:

There is one more practice worth naming specifically for lifelong learning: the habit of learning from failure. Every significant failure contains information that success cannot provide. The student who, after every major setback, takes twenty minutes to write honestly about what happened, what their role was in it, and what they would do differently, is turning every failure into a development investment. The habit of honest postmortem reflection is one of the highest-return practices available, and it is entirely free.

Extend that practice to successes too. After things go well, ask why they went well. What specifically did you do? What could you repeat? What could you build on? The student who learns systematically from both failure and success develops at a rate that surprises everyone around them, including themselves.

Apply this to everything you want to develop. Not just academic skills, but interpersonal skills, professional skills, even the intangibles themselves. Build with intention. Seek feedback. Focus on your weakest areas rather than always reinforcing your strengths. The student who is willing to be genuinely bad at something new, to persist through the discomfort of incompetence long enough to become capable, develops a capacity for growth that compounds over a lifetime.

REAL TALK

Marcus Aurelius wrote his Meditations as a private journal, notes to himself about how to live and lead, written over years of governing the Roman Empire. He was not writing for an audience. He was doing the work of deliberate self-development in writing. The practice of writing honestly to yourself, not for likes or validation, but for clarity and accountability, is one of the most powerful personal development tools available. It costs nothing. It requires only honesty and consistency. Start today.

Element Five: Civic and Community Relationships

The community involvement that most reliably produces lasting professional benefit is the involvement done for non-professional reasons: because you genuinely care about something, not because of how it looks. When you show up consistently for a cause you truly believe in, people see that you are real. They trust you differently. They introduce you to others. They vouch for you. And because the work is genuinely meaningful to you, you bring your full self to it.

Luke invested four years in civic organizations before being invited to a professional opportunity representing a major milestone. Four years of showing up, contributing, building trust. Brad quit the Chamber of Commerce within a year because he had not seen a measurable return. He missed the point entirely. Do the civic work because it matters. Invest consistently enough that the community comes to genuinely know and trust you. Everything else follows from that.

For students, civic engagement might look like sustained involvement in a cause, neighborhood, or organization you genuinely care about. The keyword is sustained. Showing up once does not build anything. Showing up every time, for months and years, builds the kind of credibility and trust that turns community involvement into one of the most productive parts of your life.

THINK ABOUT IT

Draw five columns, one for each element of Kāla. In each column, write what you currently do in this area and what you genuinely wish you were doing. The gap between those two things is your growth map.

Pick one area where the gap is most significant. Commit to one specific, manageable change this week. Make it real and do it.

Integration, Not Balance

Perfect balance across these five elements is not the goal. There will always be seasons when one element rightfully dominates. The goal is integration, a life in which these elements are connected and mutually reinforcing rather than competing. Avery, one of the most successful people I interviewed, did not separate her community involvement from her professional development. Her genuine investment in her community created the relationships that sustained her business. Her professional life and her community life were one integrated whole. When the different parts of your life pull in the same direction, the forward momentum is something remarkable.

The integration you build now, in high school, becomes the template for how you live at every future stage. Students who learn to see these dimensions as connected, who build a life in which their learning, their relationships, their values, their community involvement, and their professional aspirations all point in the same direction, carry that integrated orientation into adulthood. That integration is one of the most consistently powerful predictors of a fulfilling and successful life.

The Kāla framework also provides a useful diagnostic tool when something in your life feels persistently off. Most people, when something is not working, assume the problem is in the most obvious place. Career going badly? Work harder. Feeling depleted? Sleep more. Relationships strained? Talk more. But often the actual problem is in a different dimension than the one that is showing the symptoms. Persistent professional stagnation is sometimes caused by a neglected inner life. Relationship difficulties are sometimes caused by a vision that has never been articulated. Physical and emotional depletion is sometimes caused by the isolation that comes from neglecting community.

When something in your life is persistently not working, look across all five dimensions of Kāla and ask honestly: which of these am I most neglecting right now? The answer is often surprising, and often points toward the actual source of the dysfunction rather than the symptomatic one. The integration of all five is what produces genuine resilience and sustainable momentum. The neglect of any one, over time, creates a cascade.

> *"The real competitive advantage is not working harder in one area. It is building a life in which every area reinforces every other area. That kind of integration is rare. And it is remarkable."*

✎ **REFLECTION, THINK, WRITE, ACT**

31. *Of the five elements of Kāla, which is most underdeveloped in your life right now? What would investing meaningfully in it look like this month?*

32. *Who are the two or three people with the greatest influence on who you are becoming? Is that influence pushing you toward the person you want to be?*

33. *What is one cause or community you genuinely care about? What would committing to it seriously, for at least a year, look like?*

34. *Are the different parts of your life currently coherent and reinforcing, or do they feel like competing compartments? What would make them more integrated?*

CHAPTER 7

Real Talk: Ten Tips for the Road

From people who have been where you are going, and want you to learn from their experience, not their mistakes.

Every person I interviewed had, at some point, been standing in a version of where you are standing now. When I asked what they wished someone had told them earlier, they were generous and specific. Here is that wisdom, translated for where you are right now.

TIP 1 **Learn how the game is played before you try to change the rules.**

There is a temptation that almost every intelligent, independent young person feels: to dismiss established ways of doing things as arbitrary or inapplicable to them. Sometimes that instinct is correct. But far more often, especially when you are new to something, the established ways exist for reasons not immediately obvious. Learn the system first. Master it. Then, from a position of genuine competence and credibility, advocate for changing the parts that genuinely need changing. The people who change things most effectively are almost always those who understood what they were changing.

TIP 2 **Get genuinely involved in things that matter to you.**

Join organizations and communities not to pad an application or signal virtue, but because genuine involvement in things you actually care about is how real relationships, real skills, and a real reputation get built. The students who are involved because they genuinely care get incomparably more out of it than those who are there for appearances. Everyone around them can tell the difference. Be the one who is actually there.

TIP 3 Don't mistake your inner circle for your whole network.

The people who love you are essential sources of support. But they cannot substitute for a broader, more diverse network. They have a natural bias toward you that makes it difficult for them to give you the honest, objective feedback you actually need. Build relationships outside your inner circle deliberately and consistently. The opportunities that most change your trajectory will almost always come from beyond the people you already know well.

TIP 4 Educate yourself beyond what is required.

The minimum is always the floor. The student who has read more broadly, explored more deeply, and thought more seriously than what was formally assigned is the one who has something original to say and demonstrates the initiative that makes people want to invest in them. Go beyond the minimum because the extra investment pays for itself many times over.

TIP 5 Learn to tell your own story.

In every important professional context you will ever enter, you will be called upon to explain who you are, what you have done, and where you are going. Most people are unprepared for this. Practice telling your story. Know what makes you specific and interesting. Know what you have overcome and what it taught you. A compelling, authentic personal narrative is one of the most powerful professional tools you will ever have.

TIP 6 **Take care of your body and your mind without negotiation.**

Sleep deprivation degrades cognitive function and emotional regulation. Poor nutrition undermines energy and resilience. Unmanaged mental health struggles compound into crises far more costly to address later. Exercise is neurological maintenance, not a luxury. Your body and your mind are the most fundamental infrastructure you have. Everything you build depends on them. Protect them seriously and consistently.

TIP 7 **Develop the habit of writing.**

Writing forces a clarity that thinking alone rarely achieves. When you write down a goal, you are forced to make it specific enough to put into words. When you write about a failure, you are forced to process it in a way that reveals what it taught you. Keep a journal. Write out your goals and revisit them regularly. Write after significant experiences. The habit of written reflection is one of the highest-return investments in self-development that exists.

TIP 8 **Look the part for where you are going.**

Research what professionalism looks like in the specific environments you want to enter and show up in a way that communicates you took those contexts seriously. The student who arrives at an informational interview or a college visit looking polished and prepared tells that person something important about their maturity before a word is spoken. You get to choose what story is told. Choose deliberately.

TIP 9 **Build something before you feel ready.**

The feeling of readiness is not a precondition for starting. It is a product of starting. Almost everyone who has built something meaningful began before they felt fully prepared, failed at things, learned, and kept building. Start something now that has real stakes and forces you to develop real judgment. The person who has actually built something walks into every future opportunity with a credibility that no credential can replicate.

TIP 10 **Boldness is a muscle. Train it daily.**

Boldness is not a personality trait. It is a skill built through practice. Every time you introduce yourself to someone you do not know, raise your hand when you are not certain, or take the initiative when waiting would be easier, you are training the muscle of boldness. It gets stronger with use. The students who practice boldness consistently during high school arrive at adulthood with a capacity for action that their more passive peers will spend years trying to develop.

A Final Word on These Ten Tips

Read through these ten tips again carefully. You will notice that none of them are about intelligence, talent, or luck. Every single one is about a behavior, something you can choose, practice, and build. That is not an accident. The research behind this book, and the research behind decades of work on human performance more broadly, points consistently in the same direction: what separates the people who build meaningful lives from those who struggle is behavior, not innate capacity.

This is the most important takeaway from everything in this chapter. You are not fixed. The person you are right now is not the person you have to be. The habits you build, the relationships you invest in, the boldness you practice, the vision you develop, all of these are choices you can make, starting today. The version of you that is possible is not a distant, hypothetical future self. It is the natural product of specific decisions, made consistently, over time.

The students who read this chapter and act on it immediately, who start practicing boldness today, who write their vision statement this week, who reach out to a potential mentor before the month is over, are already demonstrating the intangible that underlies all the others: the willingness to invest in their future before the return is visible. That willingness is the foundation of everything.

I want to close this chapter with something that every person I interviewed, without exception, confirmed: the journey is worth it. Not because it is easy or because the rewards come quickly or because there are no painful seasons. But because a life built on genuine relationships, real self-knowledge, clear direction, and intentional investment across all five dimensions is a fundamentally different kind of life from one built without those things, and the difference is visible, and real, and worth every bit of the patient, consistent work required to build it.

The people who arrived at their fifties and sixties with lives they were genuinely proud of were almost universally people who had made these investments early and kept making them. Not because they were special. Because they were intentional. That intentionality is available to you right now, today, at whatever age you are reading this. It requires only a decision to begin.

CHAPTER 8

Putting It All Together

The intangibles are not a checklist. They are a way of living. And you can start living them now.

We have covered a great deal of ground. Now let me bring it all together, not just as a summary, but as a genuine integration: a way of seeing how all the pieces relate to each other and what to actually do with them.

The core argument of everything you have read is this: the difference between people who build meaningful, successful lives and those who struggle is rarely about intelligence, talent, or technical skill. It is about the intangibles. The invisible infrastructure of habits, relationships, self-knowledge, and vision that either supports a thriving life or leaves everything feeling unstable and directionless. And the most important thing you can carry from this book is this: you are not too young to start building that infrastructure. You are at the ideal moment. The foundations you lay now compound for the rest of your life.

The Intangibles, Integrated

Relational Networking

Building genuine relationships based on trust, consistency, and contribution. Show up to give, not to extract. Invest in communities you genuinely care about. Follow through on every commitment. Build social capital slowly and protect it carefully.

In practice: invest in the relationships you already have. Invest deeply in one or two organizations you genuinely care about. Be the person who follows through. Start building your social capital account now through hundreds of small, consistent deposits.

Mentorship

Finding people who have traveled some version of the road you want to travel, and being humble and consistent enough to actually learn from them.

In practice: start with the adults already in your life. Make specific, manageable requests. Follow through absolutely on everything. Be the kind of mentee that people want to invest in: curious, reliable, humble, and genuinely grateful.

Image and Presence

Showing up in a way that accurately communicates who you are and where you are going, in person, in your environment, and in your digital presence.

In practice: be intentional about how you present yourself in every context that matters. Build a digital presence you would be proud to have anyone see. Practice genuine presence. Let your wrapper reflect the quality of what is inside.

Vision

Having a clear enough picture of who you want to become to make decisions that move you toward it rather than away from it.

In practice: write your vision statement now. Identify your core values. Make it a living document that you revisit and share with a mentor. Let your vision be the filter through which you evaluate choices.

Kāla: Intentional Living Across Five Dimensions

Investing deliberately in professional growth, personal relationships, spirituality, lifelong learning, and civic engagement so they reinforce each other.

In practice: identify the most underdeveloped element and make one specific investment in it this week. Work toward integration, a life where all five dimensions are expressions of the same values, pulling in the same direction.

One final thought on integration before we move to commitments. The most fully integrated lives I encountered in the research were not those of people who had managed to perfectly balance five separate areas of life. They were the lives of people who had found, over time, a way to express a consistent set of values across every dimension. The same core identity showed up in how they worked, how they built relationships, how they engaged with their communities, how they cared for themselves, how they pursued their spiritual and inner lives.

That consistency, not balance, but coherent identity expressed across multiple dimensions, is what makes a life feel whole rather than fragmented. And it is built through the same mechanism as everything else in this book: not in one dramatic decision, but in hundreds of small consistent choices, over years, that gradually make you a certain kind of person. The person those choices make you is the most important thing you will ever build.

The Compounding Effect

The single most important reason to start now is compounding. The relationship you build with a teacher this year might produce a recommendation that opens a door three years from now, which leads to an internship that shapes your career for decades. The habit of follow-through, built now when the stakes are low, becomes one of your most valuable professional qualities over a lifetime. The vision you develop today, rough and provisional as it may be, gives your choices a coherence that accumulates over years into something remarkable.

You are at the perfect age to start. Every year matters. Every relationship, every habit, every choice about how you show up is a compounding investment in the person you are becoming. Every year you invest is a year of compounding you keep. Every year you delay is a year of compounding you give up.

Consider the difference between two students at graduation. Student A spent high school building genuine relationships with teachers, coaches, and community members. She cultivated a mentoring relationship with a professional in a field she cares about. She developed a clear sense of who she wants to become. She built a digital presence she is proud of. Student B was equally intelligent but did none of these things deliberately. He graduated with the same credential. But Student A has something Student B does not: four years of compounded investment in her intangibles. That gap will only widen. Start compounding today.

What Consistent Practice Looks Like

The intangibles are built through practice, and practice happens in the small moments. Here is what consistent practice actually looks like, concretely.

On Monday morning, you are in class and the teacher asks a question you do not know the answer to with certainty. The temptation is to stay silent. Boldness practice says: raise your hand anyway. Say what you think, clearly, acknowledging the uncertainty. You are training the muscle.

On Wednesday, someone you respect does something generous for you, takes time to explain something, writes you a recommendation, gives you advice. You could acknowledge it briefly and move on. Follow-through practice says: write a specific, genuine note of thanks within twenty-four hours. Reference something specific from what they did. You are building social capital.

On Friday, you are tempted to skip the community organization meeting because you are tired and nothing urgent is happening there. Relational investment practice says: go anyway. Show up because showing up is what you do. You are making a deposit.

None of these moments feel significant in isolation. Each one is a small, unsexy, unglamorous act. But multiplied across months and years, across hundreds of small choices, each reinforcing a character that is showing up, following through, contributing, growing, these small practices build something that cannot be manufactured any other way.

The cumulative effect of those small practices is what the researchers call character consolidation, the process by which repeated choices in small moments gradually fix a person's character into something stable and reliable. The character that is consolidated through years of consistent small practices is the character that shows up in the high-stakes moments: the job interview, the difficult conversation, the moment of genuine temptation. You do not discover your character in those moments. You display it. The discovery happens in the small moments. The display is the natural consequence.

This is why the most powerful thing you can do right now is not to wait for a dramatic opportunity to show who you are. It is to be, in every small moment, the person you want to be. Treat the person behind the counter with genuine respect. Follow through on the commitment to the small volunteer task. Show up to the meeting when nobody would notice if you skipped it. These are not just nice behaviors. They are the actual work of building a character that will carry you through a life.

The Truth About Your Future

Nobody is coming to hand you your future. The opportunities you want, the relationships that open doors, the clarity about who you are, these are built through consistent and intentional effort, over time. There is no shortcut. There is only the work, done consistently, over years.

That is not a discouraging fact. It is a liberating one. Your future is genuinely in your hands. Not determined by the family you were born into or the school you attend. Those things shape your starting point. They do not determine your destination. Not if you are willing to do the work. The students who build lives they are genuinely proud of are not, as a rule, the ones with the most advantages at the starting line. They are the ones who figured out early that success is built from the inside out. From character. From relationships. From vision. From the willingness to do the consistent work that most people defer to some vague and never-arriving later.

In Practice: Starting This Week

Everything in this chapter can feel abstract until you translate it into a specific action this week. Here are four concrete starting points, one for each of the major themes of this book. Choose one and do it before the week is out. Do not wait until everything feels clear. Start with one thing and let momentum build.

35. Write a one-paragraph description of the person you want to become in five years. Not the job title. The person. What do they value? How do they treat people? What have they built? What kind of life are they living on an ordinary Wednesday? Write it in the present tense, as if you are already there.
36. Identify one relationship in your life that you have been taking for granted, a teacher, a family friend, a mentor figure you have not been fully present for. Send them a genuine message this week. Not to ask for anything. Just to express appreciation and reconnect.
37. Look at your calendar from the last thirty days. Where did your time actually go? Does the time allocation match the person you want to become? If not, what is one specific thing you will change this week?
38. Write down the name of one person you admire and want to learn from. Not a celebrity, someone you could actually reach. What one specific question would you most want to ask them? How can you get thirty minutes of their time?

Do not try to do all four at once. Pick the one that creates the most productive discomfort and do that one. The other three will be waiting when you are ready for them.

Your Three Commitments

Before you close this chapter, make three specific commitments:

39. Name one relationship you will invest in more deliberately in the next thirty days. Who, and what specifically will you do?

40. Identify one step toward finding or deepening a mentoring relationship. One specific person you will reach out to or one specific investment in an existing relationship.

41. Write the first draft of your personal vision statement right now, before you move on. Even rough. Even provisional. Write something real.

These three things, done consistently, compound into something extraordinary.

Welcome to being bold.

The journey starts now.

CHAPTER 9

Your Path: College, Career, or Business

There is no wrong path. There is only the path you choose with clarity, intention, and the willingness to build it fully.

The intangibles do not change based on which path you choose. The principles of genuine relationship-building, real mentorship, intentional self-presentation, clear vision, and integrated living are as relevant in a college dormitory as they are on a job site or behind a startup's first desk. What changes is the application. In this chapter I want to be specific about each of the three paths, specific enough to be practically useful for wherever you are headed.

Before we get into the specifics of each path, a note about the choice itself. Most students feel significant pressure, from parents, counselors, peers, culture, to have their path figured out and declared by a specific deadline. Some of that pressure is practical; college applications require decisions. But the anxiety around "picking the right path" often obscures the more important question: whatever path you choose, are you building the intangibles that will make it successful?

The research is clear: the intangibles matter more than the path. A student who takes the college path but neglects their relationships, their vision, and their personal development will be outperformed by a student who takes the workforce path and builds all five Kāla elements deliberately. The path sets the stage. The intangibles determine what happens on it.

I have watched students take the college path, graduate with impressive credentials, and find themselves five years out from graduation in jobs they do not enjoy and lives that feel hollow, because they never developed a genuine vision, never built the relational infrastructure that would have made the credential valuable, never found the mentors who could have helped them use their education effectively. And I have watched students take the direct workforce path, skip the credential entirely, and build remarkable professional lives because they invested ferociously in their intangibles from day one.

Path is not destiny. Intangibles are.

The College Path: Building More Than a Degree

The students who get the most out of college are almost never primarily those who earn the best grades. The students who emerge most powerfully positioned are the ones who built the most while they were there, and most of what they built was not in any classroom.

What College Actually Offers

College offers a uniquely concentrated, unusually diverse community of people all simultaneously at a stage where identity and direction are actively being formed. The peers you live and study with, the faculty you work with, the professional networks that campus creates access to, these represent an extraordinary opportunity for the relationship-building and mentorship this book is about. But that opportunity is not automatic. It requires initiative.

The majority of students move through four years of college in a relatively narrow band: the same friend group, the same patterns, the same refusal to engage with anything outside their default comfort zone. They graduate with a credential and a debt load and a relatively shallow experience of what college made available to them. The students who use college differently emerge with a genuine network, real mentors, direct professional experience, and a clearer sense of who they are. Those outcomes are built, not given.

How to Use College Intentionally

- Go to office hours consistently, not only when you need help. Build genuine relationships with faculty who are experts in things you care about. A professor who knows you well can change your trajectory in ways a perfect GPA alone cannot.
- Join one or two organizations and take on real responsibility within them. Not five where you attend meetings occasionally, but one or two where you show up every time, take on unglamorous tasks, and build genuine relationships.
- Pursue work or research experience outside the classroom every year. Students who graduate with real-world experience alongside their academic credential are in a fundamentally different position than those who only have the credential.
- Be deliberate about classmate relationships. The people sitting next to you in your junior seminar might be your most important professional contacts a decade from now.
- Declare your direction, even if tentative. Being known for having a direction is how mentors find you and how opportunities reach you.

What College Cannot Do for You

College cannot give you direction, self-knowledge, or the resilience that comes from navigating real difficulty. The student who arrives without any sense of what they are trying to build there will often drift for four years. Arrive with a direction. Not a perfect plan, a direction. Know why you are there and what you are trying to build.

College also cannot substitute for the deliberate development of the intangibles. The degree is a credential. The intangibles are the infrastructure that determines what you build with it. Many students who leave college with impressive credentials find themselves surprised by how much of their success, or struggle, is determined by things they were never taught in class. You already know what those things are. You have been reading about them for the past eight chapters. Build them, in college and before.

There is one specific college trap worth naming explicitly: the trap of treating college as a four-year pause from real life. Some students approach college as a protected period, a time to figure things out, to enjoy the social environment, to put off the real decisions until graduation approaches. That approach is understandable. College is often the first time young people have significant freedom, and that freedom is genuinely exciting. But treating it primarily as a pause rather than an investment is one of the costliest mistakes a college student can make.

The students who use college most effectively are those who treat it, from day one, as the first stage of the rest of their lives. They take their relationships seriously from the first week. They seek out faculty connections from the first semester. They pursue experience outside the classroom from the first year. They develop their vision actively during their time there, rather than waiting until senior year to start figuring out what they want. The four years of college are the highest-density opportunity for intangibles development that most people will ever have. Use them fully.

> **THINK ABOUT IT**
>
> Before college, write down three things you want to have built by graduation: a genuine mentoring relationship with a faculty member in your field, at least one significant work or research experience outside the classroom, and a clearer picture of what you want to do in your first two years after graduation. Keep that list somewhere visible. Let it guide your choices for four years.

The Workforce Path: Building a Career from the Ground Up

Heading directly into the workforce after high school is not the wrong path. It is a path that rewards the intangibles just as richly as any other, in some ways more directly and immediately. Here is what the workforce actually rewards early: showing up reliably, taking initiative, building genuine relationships, and presenting yourself as someone who takes their work seriously. None of those things require a college degree. All of them are intangibles.

The students who are most successful on the workforce path understand something early: their first job is not their destination. It is where they build the track record, skills, and reputation that open the next door. The first job is not something to endure. It is something to mine, for relationships, for learning, for evidence that you are someone worth investing in.

Making the Most of Your First Job

The first job is not your destination. It is where you build the track record, relationships, and reputation that open the next door. Here is how to build:

- Be the most reliable person in the room. Show up on time. Follow through on everything without needing to be chased. This sounds basic because it is basic. And it is astonishingly rare.
- Take initiative proactively. Look around and ask: what needs to be done that nobody is doing? Then do it.
- Build relationships with people at every level. The people who have been there longer can teach you things no training program can.
- Find a mentor inside the organization. Almost every workplace has people willing to invest in younger colleagues who show initiative and respect.
- Never stop learning. Take every training opportunity available. Seek out additional learning in your field on your own time.

> *"It takes time to become confident and to be perceived as trustworthy and credible. The key is the perception others have of you. Never stop learning."* , Declan, successful business professional

Building a Career Over Time

A career is built in stages. Each stage is primarily about building the foundation for the next one. This means your responsibility at every stage is not just to do your current job well, but to actively build the platform for what comes next. Who are you meeting? What are you learning? What is your reputation becoming? As your career develops, continue to invest in credentials: certifications, licenses, degrees pursued part-time. Never stop investing in yourself.

The workforce path also offers something the college path does not always provide: immediate, real-world feedback on your skills and character. In a classroom, the consequences of not following through are usually limited to your grade. In the workforce, they affect real people and real outcomes. That immediate feedback, engaged with honestly, is one of the most powerful growth environments available. Use it.

There is a specific advantage to the direct workforce path that is underappreciated: the clarity of feedback. In the workforce, the consequences of your choices are immediate and concrete in a way that academic environments rarely match. If you do not follow through on a commitment, a real project suffers and real people are affected. If you show up poorly to a client interaction, you see the result in the relationship. If you take initiative and it works, you get concrete evidence of your own capability.

That clarity of feedback, engaged with honestly and systematically, is one of the most powerful development environments available. The student who enters the workforce with the right mindset, who treats every piece of feedback as data about how to improve, who actively seeks out mentors and stretch assignments, who invests in their intangibles with the same intentionality a college student might, will develop more rapidly than many of their credentialed peers. The certificate of learning in the workforce is the track record. Build it deliberately.

The Entrepreneurship Path: Building Something of Your Own

Entrepreneurship is the most intangibles-dependent path of all. Almost everything that determines whether a young business survives its first few years is relational: whether people trust you enough to give you their money, whether they trust you enough to refer you to others. Before you have a track record, the primary asset you have to sell is yourself. Your trustworthiness. Your character. Your vision. Your relationships in the community you serve.

The entrepreneurs in my research who were struggling were almost always struggling with the human side more than the technical side. Not enough relationships in the community they were trying to serve. No mentor to show them the unwritten rules. The ones who were thriving had invested in those things first.

Starting Your Business Life Now

- Build genuine relationships in the communities you eventually want to serve. Every genuine relationship built now is a potential client, referral, or supporter when you are ready to launch.
- Find mentors who have built businesses and are willing to share honestly what they learned.
- Start small projects with real customers and real stakes now. A side project with real skin in the game is the most valuable entrepreneurial education available.
- Develop your vision for what you want to build, the community you want to serve, the impact you want to have, the kind of business you want to run.

The Patience Paradox

Building anything real takes longer than you think. The relationships that eventually bring your most loyal clients take years to develop. The reputation that generates word-of-mouth referrals is built interaction by interaction. Luke invested four years in civic organizations before being invited to a professional opportunity representing a major milestone. He did not quit after a year. He kept showing up, contributing, building trust. And eventually, not instantly but inevitably, the investment paid off. That patience is not passive. It is active, consistent, genuine investment over a long time horizon.

The most common mistake young entrepreneurs make is expecting the intangibles to pay off quickly. They join a community, attend a few meetings, and if no immediate business results materialize, they move on. This misunderstands how the intangibles work. They are not a quick return on investment. They are a compound interest account. The returns are slow at first, then accelerating, then remarkable. The prerequisite is patience and consistency long enough for the compounding to begin.

There is an additional challenge unique to entrepreneurship: the isolation. Building a business from scratch is inherently lonely, especially in the early stages when you have not yet built a team and the only person accountable for everything is you. The entrepreneurs in my research who handled that isolation best were those who had built community before they needed it, who had relationships with other entrepreneurs they could call when things were hard, who had mentors who had been through the lonely early stages themselves and could provide perspective, who had civic and community relationships that gave their work a context larger than their own business outcomes.

Build your community before you need it. Not as a strategy for managing isolation, but because genuine community is one of the most important things any person can have, and the time to build it is long before any particular crisis demands it. The entrepreneur who arrives at the difficult early stages of building a business with a genuine community around them is in a fundamentally different position from the one who arrives alone.

What Every Path Has in Common

Regardless of which path you choose, the people who succeed over time share certain things in common. They build genuine relationships over years. They find mentors who help them see what they cannot see alone. They show up in a way that communicates they take themselves and their work seriously. They have a clear enough vision to make decisions that move them forward. They invest in the whole person, not just the career. These are not advantages of the path. They are the products of the choices made on any path.

The best time to start building these things was during high school. The second best time is today. Every day you invest in these foundations is a day of compounding you keep. Start now. Build consistently. Trust the process.

Making the Decision: How to Choose Your Path

Some students reading this know exactly which path they are taking. Others are genuinely uncertain, and that uncertainty can feel paralyzing. Here is a framework for thinking through the decision that prioritizes what the research actually supports.

First: clarify your values and your vision before you make the decision. The right path is not the one that pays the most or carries the most social prestige, it is the one that best expresses who you are and where you genuinely want to go. A path chosen based on external validation rather than honest self-knowledge will feel increasingly wrong over time, no matter how objectively successful it looks.

Second: talk honestly with people who have taken each path you are considering. Not to gather data for a pro/con list, but to understand what those paths actually require day-to-day, what they genuinely cost, and what makes them fulfilling for the people who have chosen them. The lived reality of a path is often significantly different from how it appears from the outside.

Third: make a provisional decision and commit to it fully. You do not need certainty to begin. You need direction and commitment. The student who commits fully to a path, even a tentative one, and builds the intangibles along the way will get further and learn more than the student who waits for certainty before investing.

Whatever you choose, choose it actively. Not by default, not by inertia, not because it is what your parents want or what seemed like the obvious next step. Make a genuine decision, grounded in honest self-knowledge and clear values, and then invest in it completely. That is what being bold actually means.

✎ **REFLECTION, THINK, WRITE, ACT**

42. *Which path are you most drawn to? What is one specific thing you can do in the next thirty days to start applying the intangibles to that path?*

43. *What is the single most significant gap between where you are now and where you want to be on your chosen path? What would help you most in closing it?*

44. *Think of someone a few years further along on the path you want to take. What would you ask them if you had thirty minutes of their honest attention? Have you asked them yet?*

45. *What is the very first specific step you will take toward building your future, starting today? Write it down. Then go do it.*

Appendix: Tools, Resources, and Next Steps

Your Personal Vision Statement Worksheet

Use this space to develop your personal vision statement. Take your time. Be honest. Revise as often as you need to.

Step 1: Answer these questions without editing yourself

What kind of person do I want to be known as?

What impact do I most want to have in the world?

What does a genuinely fulfilling life feel like to me personally?

What values do I want to guide every decision I make?

Where do I want to be in five years? In ten?

Step 2: Write your first draft vision statement

Distill your answers above into two or three clear, honest sentences.

Step 3: Identify your top three core values

Integrity • Growth • Service • Courage • Loyalty • Creativity • Excellence • Compassion • Honesty • Perseverance • Curiosity • Resilience • Generosity • Wisdom • Justice

My top three core values:

The Relationship Investment Tracker

List the people you are intentionally investing in, why each relationship matters to your future, and what you are committing to do.

Relationship 1

Name / Role:

Why this relationship matters to my future:

One specific action I will take in the next 30 days:

Relationship 2

Name / Role:

Why this relationship matters to my future:

One specific action I will take in the next 30 days:

Relationship 3
Name / Role:

Why this relationship matters to my future:

One specific action I will take in the next 30 days:

Relationship 4
Name / Role:

Why this relationship matters to my future:

One specific action I will take in the next 30 days:

Relationship 5
Name / Role:

Why this relationship matters to my future:

One specific action I will take in the next 30 days:

Mentor Search Worksheet

People Already in My Life With Relevant Knowledge or Experience

My Outreach Plan

Person I will reach out to first:

Specific, time-bounded request I will make:

By when:

The 30-Day Kāla Challenge

Commit to one specific action in each dimension every week for thirty days. Write your commitments here:

Professional Growth

Personal Relationships

Spirituality and Inner Life

Personal Development and Learning

Civic and Community

Recommended Reading

These books build on the ideas in Bold Blueprint and are recommended for students who want to go deeper:

- How to Win Friends and Influence People by Dale Carnegie, the foundational text on genuine relationship-building and human communication.
- The 7 Habits of Highly Effective People by Stephen R. Covey, a comprehensive framework for intentional, principle-centered living.
- Mindset: The New Psychology of Success by Carol Dweck, essential reading on the growth mindset and why effort matters more than fixed talent.
- Grit: The Power of Passion and Perseverance by Angela Duckworth, research-based exploration of what actually predicts long-term success.
- The Alchemist by Paulo Coelho, a parable about following your vision with courage and persistence.
- Outliers: The Story of Success by Malcolm Gladwell, a thought-provoking look at the factors that shape extraordinary achievement.
- Between the World and Me by Ta-Nehisi Coates, a powerful exploration of identity, community, and building a life with intention.
- Lean In by Sheryl Sandberg, a practical and personal guide to building confidence and a career on your own terms.

- Think and Grow Rich by Napoleon Hill, a classic on the mindset and habits of success, still remarkably relevant today.
- The Power of Now by Eckhart Tolle, a guide to presence and inner grounding, relevant to the spirituality element of Kāla.
- Atomic Habits by James Clear, the most practical guide available to building the habits that make the intangibles real.

My Boldness Journal: First 30 Days

Use this space to track your daily boldness practice. Each day, write one bold action you took, however small, and what it taught you.

Days 22–30: Week Four

Day 4: What I did:

What it taught me:

Day 3: What I did:

What it taught me:

Day 2: What I did:

What it taught me:

Day 1: What I did:

What it taught me:

Days 15–21: Week Three

Day 4: What I did:

What it taught me:

Day 3: What I did:

What it taught me:

Day 2: What I did:

What it taught me:

Day 1: What I did:

What it taught me:

Days 8–14: Week Two

Day 4: What I did:

What it taught me:

Day 3: What I did:

What it taught me:

Day 2: What I did:

What it taught me:

Day 1: What I did:

What it taught me:

Days 1–7: Week One

Day 4: What I did:

What it taught me:

Day 3: What I did:

What it taught me:

Day 2: What I did:

What it taught me:

Day 1: What I did:

What it taught me:

- So Good They Can't Ignore You by Cal Newport, a counterintuitive and research-based look at what actually leads to fulfilling work.

Chapter-by-Chapter Reflection Pages

Use these pages to write your key takeaways and commitments from each chapter. Return to these pages in six months and notice how your thinking has evolved.

Chapter 1: Who Are You Becoming?

My three biggest takeaways from this chapter:

One specific behavior I am committed to changing:

What the phrase "who am I becoming?" means to me right now:

Chapter 2: Building Real Relationships

The relationship habit I most need to build:

One community I will invest in more deeply:

My honest assessment of my social capital right now:

Chapter 3: Finding Your Mentor

The name of one person I will reach out to about mentorship:

What I specifically want to learn from a mentor in my area of interest:

How I will show up as a mentee worth investing in:

Chapter 4: How You Show Up

One specific aspect of my self-presentation I will change this month:

My honest audit of my digital presence:

What genuine presence looks and feels like to me:

Chapter 5: Your Vision

My current personal vision statement (write it here, then revise):

My top three core values and how I will apply them this week:

Chapter 6: Creating Your Edge

The Kāla element I am most neglecting and my plan to invest in it:

What integration of my five dimensions looks like in my life right now:

Chapter 7–9: Real Talk and Looking Forward

The tip from Chapter 7 that hit hardest and why:

What my chosen path requires from me that I am not yet giving it:

The single most important thing I will do differently starting today:

Letters to a Young Builder

The following letters are fictional composites drawn from the voices and wisdom of the real research subjects who contributed to Being Bold and Driven. They are written as if from professionals looking back at the pivotal years of their own development, to you, standing at the beginning of yours.

From Someone Who Learned to Build Relationships the Hard Way

I spent the first several years of my professional life convinced that networking was a game, and that the only people who won it were the ones who worked the room most efficiently. I showed up to events with my elevator pitch polished, my cards ready, and my eyes scanning the room for the most useful person to meet next. I got business cards. I got introductions. I got very little else.

The shift happened when I was forced, by circumstance more than wisdom, to stay in one community for a long time. A friend convinced me to volunteer for a neighborhood organization I did not particularly care about. I showed up because I said I would. I kept showing up because I had said I would again. After about six months, I realized that I had stopped calculating and started genuinely caring. And something remarkable happened: the people around me started genuinely caring back.

The clients who have most sustained my business over the years are people I met in that organization. Not because I was strategic. Because I was real. Because I showed up when there was nothing obvious to gain. Because I cared about the work the organization was doing, and the people doing it, not just about what I could extract from the room.

Here is what I want you to know: the posture of genuine contribution, showing up to give, to serve, to add real value, is not naive. It is the most practically sophisticated approach to building a professional life that I have ever encountered. And you can start practicing it today, in the communities you already belong to. Start there. Stay there. Build something real.

From Someone Who Found a Mentor Late

I did not find my first real mentor until I was thirty-two years old. Before that, I had advisors and bosses and friendly senior colleagues. But a genuine mentor, someone who took a sustained, honest interest in my development as a whole professional, who told me hard truths without an agenda, who helped me see the gap between what I was doing and what I was capable of, that relationship did not happen until my thirties.

I am not complaining about how my career turned out. But I am clear that those first ten professional years would have looked very different with a genuine mentor in them. The unwritten rules I learned the hard way. The mistakes that cost me relationships and opportunities that I could have avoided with better guidance. The clarity of direction I finally developed at thirty-five that I could have started building at twenty.

You are reading this at an age where that relationship is still available to you before you need it urgently. Before the stakes are high and the mistakes are costly. Please take that opportunity seriously. Find someone who has been where you want to go and who is willing to be honest with you about what it requires. Ask with genuine curiosity and real respect. Show up prepared. Do what they suggest and report back. And then stay in that relationship long enough to let it do the work it is capable of doing.

The mentor you build a relationship with now might still be in your life at fifty. That is not a transaction. That is one of the most valuable things a human life contains.

From Someone Who Learned to Take Care of Themselves

For the first decade of my professional life, I treated my body and my mental health as obstacles to productivity. Sleep was something you did when you had run out of other options. Exercise was a luxury for people who were not working hard enough. Stress and anxiety were just the cost of taking your ambitions seriously. I was wrong about every single one of those things.

The breaking point came when a doctor sat across from me and explained, with some firmness, that I was heading toward consequences that were not negotiable. That conversation was the most useful professional intervention I ever received, though it had nothing to do with my career. I had been treating my body like a machine to run at maximum capacity indefinitely. It had finally pushed back.

Here is what I know now that I did not know then. Sleep is not a weakness. It is neurological maintenance. The work you do on eight hours of sleep is qualitatively and quantitatively different from the work you do on five. The judgment calls you make when you are rested are different from the ones you make when you are depleted. The emotional regulation you have access to when your basic needs are met is completely different from what is available when they are not.

Take care of yourself with the same seriousness that you take your ambitions. Not as a reward for working hard enough, but as the infrastructure that makes working hard possible and sustainable. The person who arrives at thirty or forty with their health intact, their relationships intact, and their inner life stable is in a fundamentally different position from the one who has burned through all of those things in pursuit of short-term productivity. Build to last. Take care of the builder.

From Someone Who Learned What Boldness Actually Means

When I was your age, I thought boldness was loudness. The loudest voice in the room. The most impressive entrance. The biggest claims about what you were going to do. I mistook performance for courage.

What I discovered, slowly, over years of watching people build things that lasted versus things that collapsed, is that real boldness is almost never loud. It is the quiet decision, made consistently, to do the work that needs to be done before anyone is asking you to do it. To invest in a relationship before there is anything obvious to gain from it. To develop a vision before the path is clear. To ask for help before you are in crisis. To follow through on the small commitment nobody would have noticed if you had let it slide.

That kind of boldness is not glamorous. It does not make for a dramatic story. But it is the kind that builds something real, and keeps building it, through every season, the exciting ones and the grinding ones and the ones where you genuinely wonder whether any of it is worth it. And it is available to every person, regardless of their personality, their background, or their circumstances. It requires only one thing: the decision to show up, fully and honestly, to the actual work of becoming who you are capable of becoming.

You have that decision available to you right now, today, in whatever moment you are reading this. Make it. Keep making it. And trust that the compounding will do what compounding always does.

From Someone Who Figured Out the Vision Thing Late

I was good at my work for years before I had any real sense of what I was trying to build with it. I was skilled, reliable, well-regarded. I moved forward through the natural progression of my field. And I kept arriving at milestones that should have felt satisfying, promotions, recognition, new responsibilities, and feeling something that I did not know how to name at the time. Hollow is the closest word I have found.

What I was missing was vision. Not a career plan, I had plenty of those. A genuine personal vision: a clear picture of who I was trying to become and what kind of impact I wanted my work to have in the world. Without that picture, I was succeeding by someone else's definition of success. And it showed, in how I felt every morning, in the decisions I made when I was not paying close attention, in the gnawing sense that something important was missing even when everything visible was going well.

I found my way to a genuine vision eventually. I built something I am actually proud of. But the years I spent busy without direction are years I cannot get back, and the compounding I lost during them is real. Please do not spend those years the same way. Do the difficult, honest, uncomfortable work of developing a real vision, grounded in your actual values, oriented toward something that genuinely matters to you, now, while you are at the beginning. The difference between a life lived with a genuine north star and one lived without one is not subtle. It is everything.

From Someone Who Wishes They Had Started Earlier

If I could give one piece of advice to every student reading this book, it would be this: start now. Not when you are more ready. Not when the path is clearer. Not when the stakes are higher or the moment feels more significant. Now. Today. With whatever you have, wherever you are, starting from exactly where you are standing.

The people I have watched build the most meaningful professional and personal lives are, almost without exception, people who started early. Not early in the sense of knowing everything or having everything figured out. Early in the sense of taking seriously, at an unusually young age, the work of building the foundations this book describes. They built relationships before they needed them. They found mentors before they were in crisis. They developed a vision before they felt ready to commit to one. They invested in their inner lives and their communities long before those investments had any obvious professional payoff.

And the compounding worked exactly the way this book describes. By the time they reached the moments when those foundations were genuinely tested, the first major failure, the career pivot, the difficult professional relationship, the season of doubt, the foundations were there. They held. The wheel did not collapse.

You are at the beginning of something extraordinary. The version of you that is possible, built from the inside out through consistent, intentional investment in the intangibles, is someone worth working toward. Start now. Do not wait. The best time to plant a tree was twenty years ago. The second best time is today.

Use these pages for any reflections, commitments, ideas, or questions this book has raised. This space belongs to you.

Six Questions Worth Returning To

These six questions are drawn from the heart of this book. They are meant to be revisited, not answered once and put away, but returned to every six months as you grow and change. Your answers will shift. That shifting is the work.

Question 1: Who am I becoming?

Not who do I want to be, but who am I actually becoming, right now, based on how I am spending my time and what I am practicing? Look at your last thirty days honestly. What kind of person are those days building?

Question 2: Who is helping me grow?

Do I have a mentor, someone with specific knowledge of the road I am trying to travel, who is willing to be honest with me? If not, who could I ask? What is stopping me from asking?

Question 3: How am I showing up?

When the people who matter most in my professional life think about me, what do they see? Am I showing up in a way that reflects who I genuinely want to be? What is one thing I would change if I could?

Question 4: Where am I going?

Can I articulate my personal vision in two or three clear, honest sentences? Does it still feel genuinely mine? Has it evolved since I last examined it? What has clarified and what has changed?

Question 5: Am I investing across all five dimensions?

Looking at the five Kāla elements, professional growth, personal relationships, spirituality, lifelong learning, civic and community, which am I most neglecting right now? What is one specific change I will make this month?

Question 6: What is the one bold thing I have been avoiding?

There is almost always one important step, the mentor I have not reached out to, the vision I have not committed to paper, the community I have not fully invested in, the relationship I have been neglecting, that I know I should take but have been avoiding. What is mine? What will I do about it, and by when?

Return to these questions every six months. Write your answers each time. Watch who you are becoming.

About the Author

Cecilia Hegamin-Younger, PhD is a professor of statistics and legal advisor with more than 15 years of experience in evaluation and data analysis. She has successfully consulted for Fortune 500 companies, educational institutions, market research organizations, and health agencies, helping them maximize productivity by developing cutting-edge strategies to support teaching, research, and professional development.

Dr. Hegamin-Younger has written extensively on economic and health issues impacting Grenada and the Caribbean. Her books include Caribbean Adolescence: The Use and Misuse of Alcohol and Public Health Concerns of the Caribbean, both of which illuminate important challenges facing communities across the region.

Being Bold and Driven, the book from which this youth edition is adapted, grew out of her nationwide research into what separates thriving professionals and business builders from those who struggle, and her conviction that those lessons belong in the hands of young people before they reach the starting line, not after they have already paid the price of learning them the hard way.

Bold Blueprint is her answer to the phrase she heard most often in those interviews: I wish someone had told me this when I was young.

Now someone is telling you.

A final thought before you begin. This book will only be as useful as the honesty you bring to it. Reading it while staying safely at a distance from the questions it raises, treating it as an interesting set of ideas rather than a genuine invitation to change, will produce exactly nothing. The students who get the most from this material are the ones who are willing to be uncomfortably honest: about where they are now, about the gap between who they are and who they want to become, about the habits and patterns they know they need to change.

That honesty takes courage. More courage, in some ways, than any single bold action. Because it means sitting with an accurate picture of yourself, not a flattering one, not a despairing one, but a clear one, and deciding, from that honest starting point, to build something better. That decision, made genuinely and revisited consistently, is the beginning of everything this book describes. It is where being bold actually starts. Not in a dramatic moment. In a quiet, honest reckoning with who you are and who you are becoming.

You are holding something real in your hands. Use it that way.

The journey starts now. Be bold.

Made in United States
Troutdale, OR
07/21/2026

51374032R00096